T0268254

Tempo

Excursions in 21st-Century
Italian Poetry

Luca Paci was born in Novara, north Italy in 1970. Paci is currently the Co-Director of the Italian Cultural Centre Wales, the Italian Film Festival Cardiff and part of the executive board of Wales PEN Cymru. For the past five years he has been teaching Italian Studies at Swansea and Cardiff University. Paci is a translingual poet, editor and translator into English, Welsh and Italian. He has published a number of essays, articles and poems in English and Italian. Among his translations are *La Ragazza Carla* / *A Girl Named Carla* by Elio Pagliarani (Troubadour, 2006) and *Bondo* by Menna Elfyn (Ludo, 2021).

Tempo

Excursions in 21st-Century
Italian Poetry

Edited by Luca Paci

PARTHIAN

Parthian, Cardigan SA43 1ED
www.parthianbooks.com
First published in 2022
© The Contributors 2022
© This translation by The Translators 2022
ISBN 978-1-913640-56-9
Editor: Luca Paci
Cover Image: 'untitled' (2019) by Ciro Agostini
Cover design by Emily Courdelle
Typeset by Elaine Sharples
Printed and bound by 4edge Limited, UK
Published with the financial support of the Welsh Books Council British Library
Cataloguing in Publication Data
A cataloguing record for this book is available from the British Library.

CONTENTS

Introduction

The highest as the lowest form of criticism is a mode of autobiography.
– Oscar Wilde

Mi accorgo che il punto di vista continua a oscillare.
– Luigi Meneghello

Contemporary Italian poetry is still a widely unknown space for the general English-speaking public. We need to go back to the 20th-century Nobel Prize winners such as Eugenio Montale and Salvatore Quasimodo if we want to see some evidence in the English readership of the vitality of this poetic tradition.

The fact that works in translation play a marginal part in the actual publishing market might be one of the reasons why such a vibrant culture of a major European country is not fairly represented.

As translingual (English and Italian) author Jumpa Lahiri wrote, 'Language is the substance of literature, but language also locks it up again, confining it to silence and obscurity. Translation, in the end, is the key.' (Lahiri, 2019).

Hopefully this anthology, in its bilingual structure, will give a little acknowledgement to the extraordinary work that translators carry out and have broader ramifications in the English-speaking culture and society, helping to recognise the unique significance of Italian poetry.

I would like to begin from a couple of simple but necessary questions.

How does one start compiling a 21st-century anthology?

In other words, what are the criteria to follow, and what kind of inclusiveness, one should aim for?

My attempt to answer these questions is the outcome of a very personal journey as a reader, teacher, poet and translator living and working in the UK for over

twenty years. My view of Italy is inevitably affected by the physical and imagined distance between myself and my country of origin.

As writer and academic Luigi Meneghello puts it, 'I realise that the point of view keeps on fluctuating.'(Meneghello, 1997). I believe that this fluctuation, pulling me physically, symbolically and intellectually from Italy to the UK and vice versa, plays a fundamental part in this investigation into contemporary Italian poetry.

If my standpoint is different, so is my judgement and perception of the culture in question. Observing events from a different angle, as from an upside down telescope, encourages comparisons and contrasts. Diversity – this key concept we are finally beginning to come to terms with – becomes a very tangible factor.

Over the years I have become intensely aware of the linguistic, cultural, sociological and political differences as well as points of contact between Italian and Anglo-American culture. I have also experienced the power of poetry's seemingly elusive yet penetrating and flexible forms, and its capacity to engage with matters such as identity, culture, society, sex, race and politics.

I am persuaded that poetry has its own epistemic value and cannot be read in distraction: it requires the full intellectual and emotional intelligence of the reader as well as their sense of empathy. Poetry is an essential tool to understand and question at a deeper level events, feelings and attitudes of present and past, recognising the complexity of reality in a radically different way.

The French philosopher Gaston Bachelard talks about poetry as *reverberation*, a mental posture, thanks to which things and events are not linked by causality or logic but rather by their individual and pictorial significance where 'the reader is asked to consider an image not as an object ... but to seize its poetic reality.' (Bachelard, 1994).

Contemporary Italian poetry explores the linguistic practices of a country conscious of its many dialects and minority languages; its formidable strengths and tensions. The authors chosen for this anthology offer an extraordinary range of styles, tones, approaches, ways of looking at the world and ways of representing it.

It is a selection of major poets from different backgrounds: academics, working-class writers, editors, journalists, spoken-word performers, travellers and professional translators. Each voice has its unique accent, poetics, style and subject.

This poetry is not afraid to interrogate itself and its contradictions. Part of it is experimental and daring, multilingual and asemic. It probes the very possibility of language and its unconscious, asking questions on its ontology, status, and territory. It expresses itself in a form where past and present often collide and reconcile, memory and trauma are expressed in new and deconstructed types of lyricism. It is a poetry that is at times self-translated (in fact most of the poets are also translators) and translingual. Transparent and intricate, it is multifaceted and never clichéd.

Sometimes verses are constructed like an installation, at other times they are elemental. These are poems that criticise the language of power and reach for the people at the margin of the new global economy (women, the disabled, transgender people, migrants) and explore, with bold originality, the experience of separation and exclusion.

Here one can find a distinctive depth and profound understanding of suffering, a constant search of an interior space which goes beyond the Catholic façade which forms a large part of Italian 'religiosity'.

There is a lot to learn about contemporary Italy in these verses often 'embodied' in performance poetry and physically reflecting the distress of a wonderful and troubled nation still in search of identity.

Luca Paci
Cardiff, 2022

ANTONELLA ANEDDA

Antonella Anedda is a poet, academic, and translator born in Rome from a Sardinian family in 1955. She has worked as an art specialist for the Ethnographic Museum in Rome and taught at the University of Siena. She now teaches contemporary Italian literature at the University of Lugano. In 2019, she was awarded an honorary PhD by the University of Paris Sorbonne IV.

The poetry of Anedda asks fundamental questions about suffering, the sense of the tragic, war, and time. Moreover, all her work can be seen as an insightful reflection on how identity and cultural difference are formed by the language(s) we speak.

Anedda is the author of several poetry collections including: *Residenze invernali* (Crocetti Editore, 1992); *Notti di pace occidentale* (Donzelli, 1999); *Il catalogo della gioia* (Donzelli, 2003); *Dal balcone del corpo* (Mondadori, 2007); *Salva con nome* (Mondadori, 2012) and *Historiae* (Einaudi, 2018). She has written a number of essays: 'Cosa sono gli anni' (Fazi, 1997); 'La luce delle cose. Immagini e parole nella notte' (Feltrinelli, 2000); 'La lingua disadorna' (L'Obliquo, 2001); 'Tre stazioni' (Lieto Colle, 2003); 'Come solitudine' (Donzelli, 2003); 'La vita dei dettagli. Scomporre quadri, immaginare mondi' (Donzelli, 2009); 'Isolatria. Viaggio nell'arcipelago della Maddalena' (Laterza, 2013); and 'Geografie' (Garzanti, 2021).

TRANSLATOR

Jamie McKendrick is a poet and translator. He is the editor of *The Faber Book of 20th-century Italian Poems* (Faber, 2004). He edited and translated *Archipelago* (Bloodaxe, 2014); a wide selection of Anedda's poetry, which won the John Florio Prize for translation in 2016. He has also translated Valerio Magrelli's poems for *Tempo*.

VI

Non esiste innocenza in questa lingua
ascolta come si spezzano i discorsi
come anche qui sia guerra
diversa guerra
ma guerra – in un tempo assetato.

Per questo scrivo con riluttanza
con pochi sterpi di frase
stretti a una lingua usuale
quella di cui dispongo per chiamare
laggiù perfino il buio
che scuote le campane.

***

C'è una finestra nella notte
con due sagome scure addormentate
brune come gli uccelli
il cui corpo indietreggia contro il cielo.

Scrivo con pazienza
all'eternità non credo
la lentezza mi viene dal silenzio
e da una libertà – invisibile –
che il Continente non conosce
l'isola di un pensiero che mi spinge
a restringere il tempo
a dargli spazio
inventando per quella lingua il suo deserto.

La parola si spacca come legno
come un legno crepita di lato
per metà fuoco
per metà abbandono.

VI

This language has no innocence
– listen to how speeches break up
as if also here there were a war
a different war but war
all the same – in a time of drought.

And so I write with reluctance
with a few dry stumps of phrases
boxed into humdrum language
which I arrange so as to call out
down there as far as the dark
that sounds the bells

***

There's a window in the night
with two dark shapes asleep
dun as birds
whose bodies draw back against the sky.

I write with patience
to the eternity I don't believe in.
Slowness comes to me from silence
and from a freedom – invisible –
which the mainland's unaware of
– the island of a thought which spurs me
to rein in time
to give it space
inventing the desert for that language.

The word splits like wood
like a piece of wood cracked on one side,
part the effect of fire
part of neglect.

Translation by Jamie Mckendrick

Esilii

...plenum exiliis mare, infecti caedibus scopuli.

Tacito, *Historiae* I, 2

Oggi penso ai due dei tanti morti affogati
a pochi metri da queste coste soleggiate
trovati sotto lo scafo, stretti, abbracciati.
Mi chiedo se sulle ossa crescerà il corallo
e cosa ne sarà del sangue dentro il sale.
Allora studio – cerco tra i vecchi libri
di medicina legale di mio padre
un manuale dove le vittime
sono fotografate insieme ai criminali
alla rinfusa: suicidi, assassini, organi genitali.
Niente paesaggi solo il cielo d'acciaio delle foto,
raramente una sedia, un torso coperto da un lenzuolo,
i piedi sopra una branda, nudi.
Leggo. Scopro che il termine esatto è *livor mortis*.
Il sangue si raccoglie in basso e si raggruma
prima rosso poi livido infine si fa polvere
e può– sì– sciogliersi nel sale.

Exiles

...plenum exiliis mare, infecti caedibus scopuli.

Tacitus, *Historiae*, I, 2

Today I think – among the many dead – of the two
found a few yards from this sunny coast
beneath a ferry, in a tight embrace.
I wonder if coral could grow from their bones,
what the sand would do to their blood.
So I study – look among the old books
of forensic medicine my father has
for a manual where the victims
are photographed alongside the criminals
pell-mell: suicides, assassins, genital organs.
No landscape, just the steel sky of the photo,
occasionally a chair, a sheet-covered torso,
feet sticking out from a gurney, naked.
I read. I find the proper term is *livor mortis*.
Blood gathers in the lower regions and clots
first red then livid bluish till it turns to dust and so,
yes, may well eventually dissolve into the sand.

Translation by Jamie Mckendrick

Lacrime

Rileggendo il sesto libro dell'*Eneide*
davanti a questo lago artificiale coi resti di una chiesa
raggiungibile ormai soltanto in barca
penso a come resista nei secoli
l'immagine della casa dei morti,
a quanto desiderio spinga i vivi nella gola degli inferi
solo per simulare un abbraccio impossibile,
a come le mani che penso di toccare siano rami
di lecci, querce, abeti – alberi di natale,
specie inusuale in queste terre.
Nel vecchio paesaggio c'era il fiume
dove le donne andavano a lavare.
Stendendo le lenzuola sulle pietre
raccontavano di come le ombre delle madri
scendessero a turno dalla rupe solo per asciugare
le lacrime che continuavano a colare.

Tears

Rereading the sixth book of the *Aeneid*
in front of this artificial lake with the ruins
of a church only reachable by boat
I think how this image – the house of the dead –
has endured for centuries, and how
desire goads the living into the jaws
of the underworld only to simulate
an impossible embrace, and how the hands I hope
to touch are branches of holm oaks, fir trees,
Christmas trees, a species rare in these parts.
In the antique landscape there was a river
where women went to wash their things.
Laying out the sheets over the stones
they told how the shades of their mothers
would take turns to climb down from the rock
to dry the tears that continued to flow.

                              Translation by Jamie Mckendrick

Limba

Non tenes baùle 'e istrisinare in supr'e nie
Ma unu cane a trémula in s'iscuriù

Limba-matre ses triste
S'azu s'inniéddigat in sa sartàine

Sa mùghit'anziat
Sos ventos si coffundent.
Eolo survat et Babele s'isparghet.

Fiza-limba tràchitas a ghineperu
Una tremita tua naschinde
Est ch'astula de livrina in mes'a isteddos

et sas nues, sas nues a sa thurpas fughint
iscanzellande dae chelu onzi zenìas.

Tongue

You own no coffin to drag across the snow,
just a dog shivering in the dark.

Mother-tongue you're heavy-hearted;
garlic blackens in the copper pan.

A low drone rises from the hearth.
Winds tangle random and athwart.
Aeolus blows but Babel's left alive.

Daughter-tongue: creak of the juniper.
Your shudder at birth's a shard chipped off
a storm among the planets

and the clouds, the clouds blindly race
obliterating from the skies
all trace of lineage.

Translation by Jamie McKendrick

Anatomia

Dice un proverbio sardo
che al diavolo non interessano le ossa
forse perché gli scheletri danno una grande pace,
composti nelle teche o dentro scenari di deserto.
Amo il loro sorriso fatto solo di denti, il loro cranio,
la perfezione delle orbite, la mancanza di naso,
il vuoto intorno al sesso
e finalmente i peli, questi orpelli, volati dentro il nulla.
Non è gusto del macabro,
ma il realismo glabro dell'anatomia
lode dell'esattezza e del nitore.
Pensarci senza pelle rende buoni.
Per il paradiso forse non c'è strada migliore
che ritornare pietre, saperci senza cuore.

Anatomy

A Sardinian proverb has it that the devil
is indifferent to bones, perhaps because
skeletons radiate a deep peacefulness
laid out in display cases or desert landscapes.
I love their smiles composed entirely of teeth,
their skulls, the grace of their eye-sockets, the lack
of a nose, the void around their sex
and finally the hair, mere tinsel, blown away.

It's not a taste for the macabre
but the bald realism of anatomy,
praise for exactitude and order.
To consider ourselves without skin
makes us virtuous. There's perhaps no better
route to heaven than returning to stone,
knowing ourselves to be heartless.

Translation by Jamie McKendrick

FRANCO BUFFONI

Franco Buffoni was born in Gallarate in 1948 and now lives in Rome. As well as being a poet and translator, he is a professor of literary criticism and comparative literature. His poems, often autobiographical, reflect on (queer) identity, the sense of separation and the experience of feeling an outsider, memory and loss. In 1989 Buffoni founded *Testo a Fronte*, a journal that he still edits, dedicated to the theory and practice of literary translation and published by Marcos y Marcos.

Buffoni's poetry books include: *Suora Carmelitana* (Guanda, 1997); *Il Profilo del Rosa* (Mondadori, 2000); *Guerra* (Mondadori, 2005); *Noi e loro* (Donzelli, 2008); *Roma* (Guanda, 2009); *Jucci* (Viareggio Award, Mondadori, 2014); and *Avrei fatto la fine di Turing* (Donzelli, 2015). Two of his full-length collections have been published in the United States and France. As a novelist he also published *Più luce, padre* (Sossella, 2006); *Zamel* (Marcos y Marcos, 2009); *Il servo di Byron* (Fazi, 2012); *La casa di via Palestro* (Marcos y Marcos, 2014); and *Il racconto dello sguardo acceso* (Marcos y Marcos, 2016); *Due pub, tre poeti e un desiderio* (Marcos y Marcos, 2019); and *Silvia è un anagramma* (Marcos y Marcos, 2020).

TRANSLATORS

Moira Egan is an American poet and translator based in Rome where she teaches creative writing.

Geoffrey Brock is the author of three books of poetry, the editor of *The FSG Book of Twentieth-Century Italian Poetry*, and the translator of various books, most recently Giovanni Pascoli's *Last Dream* and Giuseppe Ungaretti's *Allegria*. He teaches at the University of Arkansas.

Justin Vitiello grew up in New York City and lived for many years in Philadelphia where he taught Italian at Temple University involving himself with various local anarchist activities. He was a published poet and linguist. He died on October 17, 2013.

Jacob S. D. Blakesley is an American translator of fiction and poetry who teaches at the University of Leeds, where he co-directs the Leeds Centre for Dante Studies. He won a 2018 NEA Literature Translation Fellowship for a project on translating the modern experimental Italian poet Edoardo Sanguineti.

Vorrei parlare a questa mia foto

Vorrei parlare a questa mia foto accanto al pianoforte,
Al bambino di undici anni dagli zigomi rubizzi
Dire non è il caso di scaldarsi tanto
Nei giochi coi cugini,
Di seguirli nel bersagliare coi mattoni
Le dalie dei vicini
Non per divertimento
Ma per sentirti davvero parte della banda.
Davvero parte?
Vorrei dirgli, lasciali perdere
Con i loro bersagli da colpire,
Tornatene tranquillo ai tuoi disegni
Alle cartine da finire,
Vincerai tu. Dovrai patire.

I'd like to talk to this photo of me

I'd like to talk to this photo of me next to the piano,
To the eleven-year-old boy with flaming cheeks,
Tell him it's not worth it to get so caught up
In games with his cousins,
To go along with them, brick-bombing
The neighbours' dahlias –
Not for fun
But just to feel a real part of their gang.
Really? A part?
I'd like to tell him, Leave them alone
with their targets,
go back quietly and finish your drawings,
your maps. This way,
you will overcome. You'll have to suffer.

Translation by Moira Egan

19

Da Marte dio crudo della guerra

Da Marte dio crudo della guerra
La voglia di legare il cadavere al carro
E di trascinarlo ogni mattina,
Da Mercurio l'idea di piantarla
E di farselo pagare.
Perché tutto prima o poi diventa musical
Carta da gioco figurina,
Hitler e il Feroce Saladino
Dracula l'impalatore.
E senza più coscienza di dolore.
Non c'è voce nelle pietre
Né parola che diventi carne o sangue.
(All'asta battuta da Bolaffi
Curioso il timbro a cuore o a C
Apposto a Firenze in ricezione
Sulle due lettere dal campo alla famiglia
Dello studente volontario a Curtatone).

From Mars cruel god of war

From Mars cruel god of war
The desire to tie the corpse to the chariot
And drag it around each morning,
From Mercury the idea to put a stop to that
And buy the body back.
Because everything sooner or later becomes a musical
Or a collectible card or figurine
Hitler or the Fierce Saladin
Dracula the Impaler
All stripped of any awareness of suffering.
There is no voice in stones
No word that turns to flesh or blood.
(At that auction held at Bolaffi,
Those intriguing heart-shaped or 'C' postmarks
Stamped after their arrival in Florence
On two letters sent from the field to the family
Of a student volunteer at Curtatone.)

Translation by Geoffrey Brock

***

Al canto in cerchio sincopato
Delle lingue desinenziali
Opporre il vacuo suono inane
Dell'ex lingua di Chaucer,
Restando perplessi al palato
Per l'u che fugge e diviene vi doppia
E la erre che non si riconosce più.
Saperne di più si dovrebbe
Del destino di desinenze
Quali splendida l'*en* del plurale,
Limpidi licheni sotto ghiaccio,
Lucerne in bacheca, orari da museo.

To the English Language

Chanting in the syncopated loops
Of the conjugated languages
To oppose the inane hollow thuds
Of the ex-tongue of Chaucer
Still perplexed in the palate
As the «u» escapes and doubles
And you can't hear the «r» any more…
One should know more about
The destiny of verb endings –
How splendid, that «en» of the plural!
Limpid lichens under ice,
Bulletin board lamps, museum schedules.

Translation by Justin Vitiello

'Sodomito,' vergò un giovane collega

'Sodomito,' vergò un giovane collega
Sotto una volta della Domus Aurea
Accanto al nome Pinturicchio
Autografo, come la sua invidia.
Vi si calavano i giovani pittori
E poi strisciavano fino a quei colori
E rilievi con stucchi. Lavoravano
Per ore con poca luce e pane
Tra serpi civette barbagianni
E poi vergavano la firma
Erano accesi i loro sguardi vigili
E sguaiati. Erano maschi.
Pinturicchio, definì Del Piero l'avvocato
Nel momento del massimo fulgore.

'Sodomite,' a young colleague scribbled

'Sodomite,' a young colleague scribbled
under the vault of the Domus Aurea
next to the name Pinturicchio
A signature bearing his envy.
The young painters lowered themselves
Down and then crawled up to those colours
And stuccoed reliefs. They worked
For hours with little light and bread
Among snakes and screech owls
And then they scribbled the signature
Their vigilant gazes flushed
And coarse. They were manly.
Agnelli defined del Piero Pinturicchio
at his moment of highest splendour.

Translation by Jacob S. D. Blakesley

Com'era il mondo dove sbarcò Enea

Com'era il mondo dove sbarcò Enea
Al di sotto del piano di campagna?
Rimosso lo strato di cenere compatta
Appaiono ambienti d'epoca ellenistica
Già nel 79 dopo Cristo abbandonati
Per precedenti terremoti e inondazioni…
Erano tante Rome disperse nei villaggi,
Varrone già lo scrive col tono di racconto
Mons Capitolinus era chiamato un tempo
Il colle di Saturno, e cita Ennio
Come in una favola, sul colle
Saturnia era detta la città…

How was the world where Aeneas landed

How was the world where Aeneas landed
underneath the countryside?
Removing the layer of dense ashes,
Hellenistic rooms come to the surface
Already abandoned in 79 a.d.
Due to preceding earthquakes and deluges...
So many Romes were scattered in villages,
already mentioned in Varro's sober prose
Mons Capitolinus was once called
Saturn's hill, and Ennius recounts,
As in a fable, that the hill-top city
was called Saturnia...

Translation by Jacob S. D. Blakesley

DOME BULFARO

Dome Bulfaro was born in Bordighera in 1971 and grew up in Monza, where he lives today. He is a poet, teacher, publisher and performer. He is the creator and artistic director of the PoesiaPresente Festival and PoesiaPresente Lab, a school of writing, poetry therapy and performance poetry. He uses the geography of human body and its motions as a living metaphor for poetry and change.

In 2013 he co-founded LIPS (Lega italiana poetry slam) and described the international and Italian slam movement in the book *Guida liquida al poetry slam* (Agenzia X, 2016).

Bulfaro was among the first to introduce poetry therapy in Italy with *Poetry Therapy Italia Magazine* (2020). Bulfaro has won several poetry prizes and his poems have been published in numerous anthologies, blogs and Italian literary magazines. Some of his work has been published in the US, Brazil, and the UK.

Bulfaro's published work includes: *Ossa. 16 reperti* (Marcos y Marcos, 2001); *Carne. 16 contatti* (D'IF, 2007); *Versi a Morsi* (Mille Gru, 2008); *Ossa Carne / Bones Flash* (Dot.com Press, 2012); *Milano Ictus* (Mille Gru, 2011); which was adapted as a crossover poetry, theatre and music performance; and *Marcia film* (Scalino, 2016).

TRANSLATOR

Cristina Viti is a translator and poet working with Italian, English and French. Recent translations include Anna Gréki's *The Streets of Algiers* (Smokestack Books, 2020); Mariangela Gualtieri's *Beast of Joy* (Chelsea Editions, 2018); and Elsa Morante's *The World Saved by Kids* (Seagull Books, 2016), shortlisted for the John Florio Prize.

Colonna vertebrale.
Reperto n° 9

In noi, s'impernia Galla Placidia, mosaico
di cellule staccate dall'arcobaleno
in noi, s'infuria Giovanna d'Arco, alla testa
di giuste, schierate ed apocalittiche, arse
vive per le stregonerie dei loro boia
in noi, il tempo ha succhiato il midollo del mondo
per farne il geniale pozzo di San Patrizio
in noi, ruota la scala della sapienza infinita, poggia
la colonna: serpente a sonagli affamata di popoli
antichi e moderni ingoiati come patatine ed hamburger
in noi, i ruderi di coda rizza, ci ammoniscono, sotto
rimembrano l'origine animale dell'umana natura
l'istinto quadrupede di sopravvivenza, di lotta
in noi, la posizione retta è coscienza, abbiamo ricorsi
di capobranco, di capostipite, di prevaricazione
di faraone che si mantella del sole, di graffi e amore
in noi, l'amore si alimenta nell'eterna follia, il pathos
l'elettricità che grida nel nostro vertebrato cavo
può illuminare città rase, far del cupo Las Vegas
in voi, domandatevi se per lui infilzereste il vostro cuore
come spiedino, per lei intingereste la lingua nel veleno
in voi, domandatevi se sareste disposti all'adulterio
pur sapendo che quel Malatesta già vi prende le misure
domandatevi se del vostro filmato siete attori autori!
ecco, ora posso sentirti superiore, sacro, or che scalzo fin le ossa
francescano, posso anche non manifestare la tua potenza
posso essere cibo e commensale dell'ultima cena
posso anche non essere di un sesso od esemplare
posso dare all'altro quel ch'è serbato a me
ecco, cosa è realtà cosa sogno
cosa è la spina dello stare
che dolce s'incunea
nel non dire

Spinal Column.
Finding no. 9

Inside us, Galla Placidia pivots, a mosaic
of cells loosened from the rainbow
inside us, Joan of Arc is raging, at the head
of righteous, close-ranked & apocalyptic
women burnt alive for the witchcraft of their butchers
inside us, time has sucked the marrow of the world
to turn it into St Patrick's genius well
inside us the revolving stairway of endless wisdom turns,
the column rests: the rattlesnake hungering for peoples
ancient & modern that she gobbles like burgers & fries
inside us are hard-tail relics that warn us underneath,
remembering the animal origin of human nature
the four-legged instinct for survival, for fight
inside us, the righteous position is consciousness, we've
ways of the pack leader, the forefather, the forcings
of sun-mantled pharaoh, of scratches & love
inside us, love feeds on eternal madness, the pathos
the electricity howling inside our vertebrate hollow
can light up razed-down cities, turn gloom into Las Vegas,
inside you, ask yourselves would you spike your heart
on a spit for him, dip your tongue in poison for her
inside you, ask yourselves would you be game for adultery
even knowing that Malatesta's already sizing you up
ask yourselves are you the acting authors in your own film!
there, now I can feel you as superior, sacred, now that barebone
scraped, Franciscan, I can also not manifest your might
I can be food & sharing guest at the last supper
I can also not belong to any sex or sample
give to the other what's been kept for me
there, what is reality what dream
what is the spine of abiding
wedging itself gently
into not-telling

Translation by Cristina Viti

31

Carnificazione.
Contatto n° 0

Mai immaginato avrei mai mai che il naso
un giorno avrebbe offeso l'occhio, l'occhio
nel vuoto avrebbe paralizzato i suoi tic
mai immaginato avrei mai che quei denti
potessero ringhiare alla propria mano, la mano
destra un giorno accoltellasse la sua sinistra
mai immaginato avrei l'anima mia finisse
per sgusciare la sua testa, la testa
un giorno si sarebbe scontrata con le ginocchia
mai eppure è successo che il corpo di tutti
s'issasse sulla croce con le sue stesse vene, le vene
blu di ogni uomo votassero il proprio collasso!
le vene blu di ogni uomo votassero il proprio
collasso! il blu d'ogni uomo votasse: collasso!

Fleshing.
Contact no. 0

Never imagined never I'd never the nose
would one day offend the eye, the eye
paralyse its own tics in the void
never imagined I'd never those teeth
could snarl at their own hand, the right hand
one day take a knife to its own left
never imagined I'd never my own soul would end
up slip-shelling its own head, the head
one day crash into the knees
never & yet it's happened everyone's body would
hoist itself onto the cross with its own veins, the blue
veins of each man vote their own collapse!
the blue veins of each man vote their own
collapse! the blue of each man vote: collapse!

Tallone del capogiro.
Contatto n° 25 (parte dx)

Come deglutire tutto il mare, farne il mucchio
che sono? Come stipare ogni voce nella punta
della matita? Come raggrumare giostre
corsie ospedaliere, nello stesso tallone
accomodare te e il padre del tuo cognome? Cantare
questo è il solo sangue che il poeta può donare
consonante dopo vocale, dissanguarsi nel tovagliolo
del bar scrivere – le poesie sono di chi se le beve –
le poesie t'affacciano nel precipizio della pulsazione
per questo canto perché nella gola nessuno del coro
mai s'estingua perché quando canto m'illudo d'incarnare
l'unica lingua canto perché io non danzi con un moribondo
tuono, canto perché quando canto solo canto sono

Spinning Head Heel.
Contact no. 25 (part right)

How to swallow the sea whole make of it the heap
that I am? How to cram each voice into the tip
of the pencil? How to clot carousels
hospital wards & into the same heel
accommodate you & the father of your surname? To sing
that's the only blood the poet can give
consonant after vowel bleeding oneself into a napkin
in a bar writing – poems belong to those who drink them up –
poems push you to face the precipice of pulse
for this I sing for no one in the choir
to ever be extinguished in the throat for when I sing I dream I'm fleshing
the one language I sing so as not to dance with dying
thunder, I sing for when I sing I'm nothing but singing

Nuca. Contatto
n° 31 (parte dx)

La fronte di mio padre è lunga otto ore
non ha capelli intorno ma irte donne
a lutto, fra gli occhi ha un cestino dove
porre baci impacchettati da troppi anni.
La fronte di mio padre è pianura al sole
ma nel resto è come noi: non finito
scabro dolore, per questo ti prego
ora padre lascia che tuo padre sia io
la mano sotto la nuca la mia
sia, padre morto, tu bambino mio

Nape.
Contact no. 31 (part right)

My father's forehead is eight hours long
it has no hair around it but bristling women
in mourning, between his eyes is a basket where
you can place kisses wrapped up for too many years.
My father's forehead is a plain in the sun
but otherwise he is like us: unfinished
rough-hewn grief, for this I beg you
now father, let your father be me
the hand under the nape, let it be mine
let it, dead father, let yourself be my child

Translation by Cristina Viti

Ictus 1.
Scheletrico di una famiglia

bello vederti morire così: / le ciocche gravide di fichi acerbi
spoglia delle vestaglie di trent'anni, / veder l'agonia dei seni gonfiarsi
nella pelle che non saremo più: / moriremo genitori, famiglia,
pescheremo uno scheletro dal ventre. / nell'ombelico il vento ha insufflato
un seme, il seme ha acceso un focolare / a cui il gelo mostrerà il suo rancore.
bella la fronte di noi due che crepa, / con gl'occhi che ci cadono in frantumi,
di una bellezza senza latte, un latte / senza labbra, labbra che già decretano
non più due: abbiamo rubato un uovo / dal nido, tutta la notte a guardare
con la candela il becco nella crepa / nella crepa il passero rotto della
nostra coppia con i baci contati, / la nostra selvatica perfezione
due petali di pesco sul tavolo, / è questa la reciproca soglia: un feto
non è che una fiamma nella nostra ombra, / fosse restato lì, senza parlare
coi petali sul tavolo, irrisolto, / noi fossimo restati nell'orto ombre
del feto, dando retta alle ortiche, / senza pensare a quanto lutto ha in seno
la primavera, quanti volti sfumano / in noi stessi e dal fianco ci sanguinano
nel tempo steso in avanti, così / abbiamo riconosciute nell'ape
per sempre stesa a terra le sei nostre / braccia conserte, la bellezza inerte.

crollare come due angeli feriti, / culo all'aria la bava sul cuscino
le lampade di notte tutte intorno / chine e mute sul letto del delitto
a scaldarci, avvolti in lenzuola spiumate / col coltello affondato tra le gambe
svenuti di piacere nel sonno del tempo; / ci scoprissero così ci direbbero
morti, non chi ci ha scelti, lui sa / che dormiamo sotto una coltre di farfalle
con in bocca neve rossa – feto / io sono troppo giovane per sciogliermi
in madre, rinunciare alla mia scorza / di melagrana spaccata nel pube –
vuoi abortire? che cosa vuoi fare? / dormire nel palmo della tua mano
tornare rigurgito d'universo / nel rantolo dei fior di pioppo, nel gambo
spoglio che ci graffia comprendere / chiaramente il cantato degli uccelli.
tu sarai il tuo ultimo richiamo prima / di rinascere, dimenticherai
chi cosa sei stato prima degl'occhi; / nell'ombra crederai che noi due siamo
tuoi genitori, noi lo crederemo / con te, smemorati lo crederanno
tutti, staccati dalla luce gravitiamo / verso il colore delle ossa, del dubbio,

Ictus no. 1.
Bone Structure Of A Family

beautiful to see you dying like this: / locks heavy with green figs
disrobed of the thirty years, / to see the agony of the breasts as they swell
inside the skin we will no longer be: / we shall die as parents, a family,
we shall fish a skeleton from the womb. / the navel wind-planted with
a seed, a seed that sparked a hearth / to which frost will show bitterness,
beautiful this forehead of ours as it cracks, / our eyes falling to pieces,
of a beauty without milk, a milk / without lips, lips already decreeing
no longer two: we've snatched an egg / from the nest, all night watching
with a candle the beak in the crack / in the crack the broken sparrow of our
couple with counted kisses, / our wild perfection
two peach blossom petals on the table, / that's the mutual threshold: a foetus
is but a flame inside our shadow, / had it stayed there, without speaking,
unresolved, its petals on the table, / had we stayed in the kitchen garden as
$$\text{shadows}$$
of the foetus, going along with the nettles, / not thinking how much loss
spring carries in her breast, how many faces fade / into us & bleed from our
$$\text{hip}$$
into stretched forward time, so it was / we recognised inside the bee forever
stretched out on the ground our own six / folded arms, beauty at rest.

collapsing like two wounded angels, / arse in the air drool on the pillow
night lamps all around / silently curved over the bed of the crime
warming us wrapped in ruffled sheets / the knife deep between our legs
fainted with pleasure in the sleep of the time; / found like this we'd be
$$\text{pronounced}$$
dead, not by the one who chose us, he knows / we sleep under a cover of
$$\text{butterflies}$$
with red snow in our mouth – foetus / I'm too young to melt
into mother, to renounce my bark / of pomegranate split at the crotch –
have an abortion? what do you want? / to sleep in the palm of your hand
to be a backsurge of the universe / in the painting of a poplar flower,
in the bare stem that scratches us to understand / birdsong clearly.

attirati da ciò che più ci offusca; / si muore così per una stillicida
dimenticanza. si gela così / per una dimenticanza.
si gela / per dimenticanza.
sbranati dal torpore

you'll be your own last wild call before / being reborn, you'll forget
who what you have been before the eyes were; / in the shadow you'll believe us
to be your parents, we'll believe that / with you, and so, forgetfully,
will everyone, as detached from light we gravitate / to the colour of bones, of
doubt,
attracted by what darkens us most; / one dies like this through a dripping of
forgetfulness.
one freezes like this / through some forgetfulness.
one dies / through forgetfulness.
torn to pieces by torpor

Translation by Cristina Viti

41

MARIA GRAZIA CALANDRONE

Maria Grazia Calandrone is a poet, playwright, journalist, performer and novelist based in Rome. She presents cultural programmes on RAI and Corriere TV and writes literary criticism for *Poesia, il manifesto, Corriere della Sera* and *7*. She also leads poetry workshops in schools, prisons, and mental health units.

Calandrone's books include: *Pietra di paragone* (Tracce, 1998 – Nuove Scrittrici Award); *La scimmia randagia* (Crocetti, 2003 – Pasolini Award); *Come per mezzo di una briglia ardente* (Atelier, 2005); *La macchina responsabile* (Crocetti, 2007); *Sulla bocca di tutti* (Crocetti, 2010 – Napoli, Sassari and Prata Awards); *Atto di vita nascente* (LietoColle, 2010); *La vita chiara* (transeuropa, 2011); *Serie fossile* (Crocetti, 2015); *Gli Scomparsi – storie da 'Chi l'ha visto?'* (Pordenonelegge, 2016); *Il bene morale* (Crocetti, 2017); *Giardino della gioia* (Mondadori, 2019); and the autobiographical novel *Splendi come vita* (Ponte alle Grazie, 2021) which was longlisted for the Strega Prize, Italy's most prestigious literary award.

Her translated poetry appears in *Fossils* (SurVision, Ireland, 2018); *Sèrie Fòssil* (Edicions Aïllades, Ibiza, 2019 – translated by Nora Albert); and the Arabic anthology *Questo corpo questa luce* (al-Mutawassit, Damascus, 2020).

She has also written short stories, present in numerous anthologies, and edited and introduced Nella Nobili's poetry volume *Ho camminato nel mondo con l'anima aperta* (Solferino, 2018) and Dino Campana's *Preferisco il rumore del mare* (Ponte alle Grazie, 2019). In 2017, she appeared in Donatella Baglivo's documentary *Il futuro in una poesia* and in Israeli film-maker Omri Lior's *Poems With a View*. Her poetry has been translated into over twenty languages.

TRANSLATOR

Johanna Bishop translates contemporary Italian poetry, fiction, non-fiction and art criticism. Her work has appeared extensively in the bilingual review *TheFLR*, as well as in other journals and anthologies, and recent books include *Tamam Shud*, a novel by visual artist Alex Cecchetti. She lives in Tuscany.

Intelletto d'amore

La poesia è anarchica, risponde a leggi solo proprie, non può e non deve
                                            piegarsi a nient'altro
che a se stessa.
La sua legge interiore è ritmo, musica assoluta.
Questo spiega la commozione che proviamo nell'ascoltare letture di poesia
                                            in lingue a noi sconosciute.
Abbiamo l'impressione di comprendere
anche se non capiamo le parole,
perché le nostre molecole consuonano con la musica profonda della poesia,
che è la stessa in ogni lingua: un ultrasuono, un rumore bianco.
Una lingua invisibile, un ronzio nucleare
traducibile per approssimazione,
una sonorità che entra in risonanza con la parte più estranea e profonda delle
                                            nostre molecole
e col rombo primario della materia
che compone la sedia
sulla quale sediamo.
Come certa musica – penso al *Chiaro di luna* di Ludwig van Beethoven – è
                                            un linguaggio
letteralmente universale:
i poeti lo scrivono da sempre, ma le recenti scoperte astrofisiche lo
                                            confermano
con rigore scientifico, non più solo intuitivo: il nucleo più profondo di noi
è composto della stessa materia delle stelle.
Parole di Margherita Hack: «Tutta la materia di cui siamo fatti l'hanno costruita
le stelle. Tutti gli elementi, dall'idrogeno all'uranio, sono stati fatti nelle reazioni
nucleari che avvengono nelle supernovae, stelle molto più grandi del Sole, che
alla fine della loro vita esplodono e sparpagliano nello spazio il risultato di tutte
le reazioni nucleari avvenute al loro interno».
Dalle scoperte ultimissime sappiamo ancora che
metà degli atomi che formano i nostri corpi è materia prodotta fuori dalla Via
                                            Lattea, viene da una distanza
        che non si può
commensurare.

Intellect of Love

Poetry is anarchic, it follows only its own laws, it cannot and must not bend
                                                                to anything
except itself.
Its inner law is rhythm, pure and simple music.
That explains why we can be moved by poetry we hear read in languages we
                                                                do not know.
We almost feel that we understand
even without grasping the words,
because our molecules ring in consonance with the deep music of poetry,
which is the same in every language: ultrasound, white noise.
An invisible language, a nuclear hum
translatable by approximation,
a sound that resonates with the deepest and most alien part of our molecules
and with the primal rumbling of the matter
that makes up the chair
we're sitting on.
Just as certain music – Ludwig van Beethoven's *Moonlight Sonata* comes to
                                                                mind – is a literally
universal language:
poets have written this forever, but recent discoveries in astrophysics confirm it
with scientific rigor, not just intuition: our deepest core
is composed of the same stuff as stars.
According to Margherita Hack: 'All the matter we are made of was built by stars.
All of the elements, from hydrogen to uranium, were formed in nuclear reactions
that take place in supernovas, when stars much bigger than the Sun explode at
the end of their lives and scatter into space the products of all the nuclear
reactions that have taken place within them'.
Very recent discoveries also tell us that
half the atoms making up our bodies are matter formed outside the Milky
                                                Way, coming from a distance impossible
to measure.
The vibration of our molecules comes into material resonance with the
                                                                vibration of the
universe,

45

La vibrazione delle nostre molecole entra in risonanza materiale con la
vibrazione dell'universo,
fin dentro l'universo sconosciuto. Questa forza
«che move il sole e l'altre stelle»
è quella che Dante chiama «amore».
La poesia intercetta il corale profondo e ininterrotto di questa forza, intona
la sua voce
al rombo delle stelle extragalattiche
e al rombo primario della materia
che compone la sedia
sulla quale sediamo.
È un oggetto fatto di parole
sempre d'amore.
E basta.

far beyond the universe we know. This force
'that moves the sun and other stars'
is what Dante calls 'love'.
Poetry tunes into the deep, uninterrupted chorus of this force, pitching its
                                                              voice

to the rumbling of extragalactic stars
and to the primal rumbling of the matter
that makes up the chair
we're sitting on.
It's an object made of words
of love alone.
That's plenty.

Translation by Johanna Bishop

L'85 è il sorriso degli amanti quando s'incontrano per caso a Fiumicino Aeroporto

Metà maggio, Roma
bella come un miraggio. Sul piano cartesiano
dell'asfalto del Corso, la tagliola del becco di un gabbiano
scatta
sul silenzio assoluto della preda, una tortorina comune. Osso giallo
su piume cinerine
arruffate. Rasoterra, una stasi irreale.

La natura si adatta al cambiamento. Ogni singola cellula di ogni corpo
vivo, obbedisce alla norma universale: ottenere il profitto maggiore
col minore dispendio di energia. Non fanno eccezione
i quattromila *Larus michahellis* (gabbiano reale mediterraneo)
che hanno colonizzato le discariche urbane. E noi, avvinti a guardare
bianchi uccelli marini cacciare
alla larga dal mare. Corpi alieni, scheggiati, malinconici come relitti.

La tortorina grigia non si dibatte, pare pronta alla fine: forse
la natura ha pietà. Forse le tortore, le gazzelle, i cervidi, forse tutte le prede
sono provviste di una ghiandola
che rilascia endorfine (anestesia, addirittura benessere); adesso che la
                                                        trappola si chiude
sopra la loro vita
mitissima. Un dolore
annunciato dalla nascita. Una paura
prevista, sopra la quale ininterrottamente
scorre il sangue della dimenticanza.
La tortorina ha smesso di aspettare.
Quello che doveva accadere, è accaduto. È docile, non piange.

Dal fondo della strada avanza l'autobus 85, che investirà la coppia,
l'assemblaggio storto
di rostro, collo e tensione

The 85 is the Smile of Lovers Meeting by Chance at Fiumicino Airport

Mid-May, Rome
lovely as a mirage. On the Cartesian plane
of the Corso asphalt, the sprung trap of a seagull's beak
snaps shut
on the utter silence of its prey, a turtle dove. Yellow bone on grey ruffled
plumage. Pressed to the ground, an unreal stasis.

Nature adapts to change. Every single cell in every body
that's alive obeys the universal rule: get the maximum possible gain
with the minimum possible outlay. This also holds true
for the four thousand *Larus michahellis* (yellow-legged gulls)
that have colonised the urban landfills. And us, we gaze entranced
at the white seabirds hunting
far out to land. Alien bodies, scudded in, melancholy as shipwrecks.

The grey turtle dove doesn't struggle, it seems ready for the end: maybe
nature is merciful. Maybe doves, gazelles, cervids, maybe all prey
are endowed with some kind of gland
that releases endorphins (anaesthesia, a sense of well-being even); at this point
when the snare snaps shut
over their lives
of gentleness. A pain
ordained from birth. A fear
foreseen, over which in a steady current
the blood of forgetting flows.
The dove is done with waiting.
What had to happen, has. It's docile, doesn't whimper.

Rolling down the street is the 85 bus, which is going to hit the couple, this
crooked assemblage
of rostrum, neck, and craniofacial
tension, unless the gull can summon the strength to take flight

49

craniofacciale, se il gabbiano non avrà forza per sollevarsi in volo
col suo muto fardello semivivo.

Stacco dell'occhio giallo. Stacco da terra, fallito. Nessuna zuffa. Il predatore di
mare sgancia la presa.

Il corpo molle della tortorina cade
in abbandono. Morta
o non ha capito
di essere salva. Tutta scossa, si riprende
sé, la bella vita
gialla di primavera. Farà un nido, s'innamorerà. Per cominciare,
zoppica e sbanda fino al marciapiede. Salva, improvvisa, perturbata sempre.
La libertà l'ha avuta
impreparata. Accogliere
la gioia, è il mestiere di tutta la vita.

with its mute half-alive burden.

Cut of the yellow eyes. Cut to lift-off, unsuccessful. There's no struggle. The
marine predator lets go.

The turtle dove's soft body falls
limp and abandoned. Dead
or unable to grasp
that it's safe. All rattled, it recovers
itself, the sweet yellow
life of spring. It will build a nest, fall in love. To begin with,
it limps and weaves its way to the kerb. Unharmed, startling, still unsettled.
                                                        Freedom caught it
unprepared. How to welcome
joy, that's the occupation of a lifetime.

                              Translation by Johanna Bishop

Pietro Maso. Senza emozione e senza rimorso

Il 17 aprile 1991 Pietro Maso, dopo tre tentativi falliti, riesce a uccidere entrambi i genitori. Non esistono contrasti gravi in famiglia, lo scopo dichiarato del matriparricida è ottenere l'eredità.

Nel febbraio 1992, presso la discoteca «Modo» di Domegliara, nasce il «Pietro Maso Fans Club». I *masiani* indossano camicia azzurra infilata entro pantaloni morbidi di colore grigio, a vita alta, blazer blu con bottoni dorati e foulard blu a pois bianchi; portano i capelli impomatati e pettinati all'indietro, la nuca rasata a V. Copiano lo stile lussuoso che Maso ha copiato da Don Johnson di *Miami Vice*.

I più estremisti legano alla vita grembiuli da macellaio schizzati di sangue e brandiscono finti coltellacci.

Nel marzo 1992, durante la partita contro la Cremonese, dalla curva Sud si alza il coro delle Brigate Gialloblu dell'Hellas Verona: «Nella vecchia Montecchìa, ia- ia-o, / Maso còpa anche sua zia, ia-ia-o, / con il cricco, cricco, crick, crick, cricco...».

La cosiddetta «massa» idolatra chi ha avuto la disinibizione di abilitare gli istinti più colpevoli e oscuri che, a istanti, abitano chiunque, ma solo in casi eccezionali come questo diventano progetti atti a modificare la realtà.

Io voglio tutto quello che voglio. Prima di tutto
il villino col giardinetto. Per avere il villino col giardinetto, devo rimuovere
la famiglia che attualmente lo abita. Essa è la mia famiglia.

Per estinguere la mia famiglia, mi servono alcuni attrezzi:
due pentole, tre amici, un tubo in ferro e un bloccasterzo.

«Qui a Cchattanooga Tennessee qquando il ssole ti ssspaca in quatro...»

Poiché i miei genitori sono restii a morire, si renderanno necessari anche una matassa di cotone e un sacchetto di nylon.
Erano benvoluti, buoni, semplici. Erano da sopprimere.

Pietro Maso: without Emotion and without Remorse[*]

On 17 April 1991, Pietro Maso, after three failed attempts, succeeds in killing both his parents. There is no serious conflict in the family, the matriparricide's stated goal is to inherit their money.

In February 1992, the 'Pietro Maso Fan Club' is founded at the Modo nightclub in nearby Domegliara. The *masiani* wear blue shirts tucked into loose, high-waisted grey trousers, blue blazers with gold buttons and blue scarves with white polka dots; their hair is slicked back, shaved into a V at the nape. They copy the swank style Maso himself copied from Don Johnson on *Miami Vice*.

The most hardcore among them tie on blood-splattered butcher's aprons and brandish fake knives.

In March 1992, during a match with Cremonese, the Hellas Verona Ultras begin chanting from the *curva*: 'In the town of Montecchìa, eeah-eeah-oh, / Maso even whacked his Aunt Maria, eeah-eeah-oh, / with a car jack, car jack, crack, crack, car jack…'.

The so-called 'masses' idolize those disinhibited enough to implement the darkest, most deplorable urges that may inhabit anyone at times, but only in exceptional cases like this one become plans that can alter the shape of reality.

I want what I want. To start with,
a nice house with a garden. To get the nice house with a garden, I must
remove the family that currently lives there. That family happens to be mine.

To eliminate my family, I will require some equipment:
two heavy pans, three friends, an iron pipe and a steering wheel lock.

'Qui a Chattanooga Tennessee quando il sole ti spacca in quattro…'

Since my parents refuse to die quickly, I will also be forced to use a wad of cotton and a plastic bag.

They were well-liked, goodhearted, simple people. They had to be terminated.

---

[*] In this poem, Maso's imagined words are interspersed with phrases from Italian ad campaigns of the 1980s and from *Miami Vice*.

«Più lo mandi giù, più ti tira su!»

Se tua madre non vuole essere cremata, il suo è un corpo che può essere riesumato. Per dire. L'omicidio va pensato, vanno valutate le concause. Avevo fallito altre volte, nell'ucciderli. La prima volta era stata colpa dell'inesperienza: avevo sistemato nel salone due bombole di gas e una centralina di luci psichedeliche, di quelle che si accendono coi rumori forti. Avevo puntato la sveglia alle 21.30, perché a quell'ora i miei guardavano la televisione. Suona la sveglia, si accende la luce e provoca la scintilla d'innesco. Sbam! Una buona idea. Avevo occluso la canna del camino con i vestiti, per aumentare la potenza d'urto dell'esplosione. Ma niente. Avevo tolto la sicura alle bombole, ma non avevo aperto le manopole e il gas non era uscito. Ingenuità. Ho dovuto spiegare a mia madre che ci facevano le bombole in salotto e i vestiti nella canna fumaria. Le sue continue richieste dovevano essere arginate. Quello che sfugge al mio controllo mi attacca. Lei, particolarmente.

«Se ho fame me la fate passare, se non ho fame me la fate venire…»

La seconda volta, il mio amico non se l'è sentita di uccidere mia madre in macchina con un batticarne.
Mi toccava farlo io. Chi non uccide il padre rimane una persona non emancipata.

«E la mamma lo sa?!»

Mi ero staccato completamente da loro, per portare a termine il mio piano. Si era ingenerato un distacco. Solo io esistevo. Gli altri erano vuoto. Mondo deserto. Ero come le chiese che hanno i demoni all'esterno. Mi dovevo proteggere. Ero sacro.

«Io ce l'ho profumato!»

Leggevo i consigli di mia madre come occasioni per umiliarmi.
Mi sembrava di capire cosa volesse trasmettermi lanciandomi certe occhiate. Occultarmi, voleva.

'Più lo mandi giù, più ti tira su!'

If your mother is against the idea of cremation, her body could later be exhumed. For example. Murder has to be thought out, you have to weigh all the factors. I'd failed on other occasions, at killing them. The first time was due to lack of expertise: down in the den I'd prepared two gas canisters and some strobe lights, the kind that are sound-activated. I set the alarm clock for 9.30 pm, since my parents would be watching TV. The alarm goes off, the lights flash and trigger an explosion. Bam! Great idea. I stuffed some clothes in the flue of the fireplace to make for a bigger blast. No luck. I'd taken the safety seal off the canisters, but forgot to unscrew them and no gas came out. Inexperience. I had to explain to my mother why there were gas canisters in the den and clothes stuffed up the chimney. Her constant nagging had to be contained. Anything outside my control is an attack on me. Especially her.

'Se ho fame me la fate passare, se non ho fame me la fate venire…'

The second time, my friend couldn't work up the nerve to kill my mother in the car with a meat mallet.
I was going to have to do it myself. If you don't kill your parents you'll never be free.

'E la mamma lo sa?!'

I'd broken off from them completely, in order to carry out my plan. A detachment had been achieved. Only I existed. Other people were empty space. A deserted world. I was like those churches with devils on the outside. I had to protect myself. I was sacred.

'Io ce l'ho profumato!'

I saw my mother's advice as attempts to humiliate me.
I thought I knew what she was trying to say with certain glances.
Conceal me, that was her plan.

«Vivi ora, la vita è breve, il tempo è fortuna»

Mia madre capiva che la stavo uccidendo. Il suo sguardo non bastò
a fermarmi. Questa è un'affermazione da rettificare.
L'odore della carne aperta
non mi ha più abbandonato.

'Live now. Life is short. Time is luck.'

My mother understood that I was killing her. Her glances were not enough
to stop me. This is a statement to be rectified.
The smell of open flesh
has never left me since.

Translation by Johanna Bishop

***

sembrava una faccenda naturale, che tu nascessi, coi muscoli crociati
in posizione
e tutto il corpo predisposto al vivere, sembrava niente

che tu cadessi
in tutto quello che incomincia
a morire

incorniciato dai fiori
e con la gola scoperta:
ecco
la vita in campo aperto,
con la rachide
tutta fiducia,

le ossa ancora cave
dei bambini, come le ossa degli uccelli

e le borchie d'ottone
poi, a riflettere il sole

sulla terra che prende colore,
dove sarai
grande abbastanza
da diventare niente
per sempre
e dire *un cuore solo non basta*
per ricambiare
la bellezza, che vedo

***

it seemed like a natural thing, for you to be born, with your cruciate muscles
                                                                    in position
and your whole body predisposed to live, it seemed like nothing

for you to fall
into everything that begins
to die

framed by flowers
and with your throat bare:
                              there
life in the open field,
with a spine
of pure faith,

the still-hollow bones
children have, like the bones of birds

and brass studs
later, to reflect the sun

on an earth that is taking on colour,
where you will be
big enough
to become nothing
forever
and say *one heart is not enough*
to repay
the beauty, that I see

Translation by Johanna Bishop

Un misterioso albero-motore

E poi un giorno c'investe
un ordigno
traslucente e radioso, che non abbiamo scelto
e chiamiamo *vita*.

L'impulso anima e flette
un suo morbido grommo di materia
viva, un insieme di organi legati – con tubicini,
cavi e percolature – a una bocca che evoca il mare.

Ma un impasto di conseguenze illogiche, di stranianti e disutili
connessioni, inverte la dialettica
di causa-effetto dell'inanimato,
se è vero che l'amore, entro i limiti dati
dalla sopravvivenza, influisce sul corpo più del pane. Intanto l'invisibile
fabbrica chimica
séguita a distillare, disseziona e sgocciola in cavità
infinitesimali
il frutto dissolto.

Dunque un giorno veniamo in possesso
del sogno della materia
che misteriosamente, come vedi, si muove
e appartiene a sé stessa e si pensa
e lentamente impara a non ferirsi.

Alla fine, un'altezza con figure.

A Mysterious Reciprocating Engine

And then one day we're hit by
an explosive device
a translucent and radiant one, that we never chose
and that we call *life*.

The pulsion animates and flexes
its own soft grume of living
matter, a set of organs tied – with little tubes,
cables and seepages – to a mouth that summons up the sea.

But a slurry of illogical consequences, of disconcerting and unfunctional
connections, inverts the cause-and-effect
dialectic of the inanimate world,
if it's true that love, within the limits set
by survival, affects the body more than bread. Meanwhile the invisible
chemical factory
carries on with distillation, dissecting and dripping
the dissolved fruit
into infinitesimal cavities.

So one day we come into possession
of the dream of matter
that mysteriously, as you see, moves
and belongs to itself and conceives itself
and slowly learns how not to harm itself.

At the end, a great height with figures.

Translated by Johanna Bishop

CHANDRA LIVIA CANDIANI

Chandra Livia Candiani was born in 1952 in Milan, where she lives today. For many years she translated Buddhist texts from English. She has also published a book of stories, *Sogni del fiume* (La biblioteca di Vivarium, 2001) and the following poetry collections: *Io con vestito leggero* (Campanotto, 2005); *La nave di nebbia. Ninnenanne per il mondo* (La biblioteca di Vivarium, 2005); *La porta* (La biblioteca di Vivarium, 2006); *Bevendo il tè con i morti* (Interlinea, 2015); *La bambina pugile ovvero la precisione dell'amore* (Einaudi, 2014); *Fatti Vivo* (Einaudi, 2017); *Vista dalla luna* (Salani Editore, 2019); and *La domanda della sete* (Einaudi, 2020).

Her latest books are *Il silenzio è cosa viva* (Einaudi, 2018) and *Questo immenso non sapere* (Einaudi, 2021). Candiani's writing style is influenced by her Buddhist practice: uncomplicated and essential, yet vigorous and emotional, as penetrating and persuasive as a soft voice. Poetry becomes a shield from pain, violence and abandonment.

Candiani regularly gives poetry classes in primary schools, as well as in hospices for people with AIDS and in shelters for homeless people. She edited, with A. Cirolla, *Ma dove sono le parole?* – poems written by children from the multi-ethnic suburbs of Milan (Effigie edizioni, 2015). She has won several creative prizes, including the Premio Montale per l'inedito (2001), the Camaiore Prize (2014), and Cultura Civile Pier Mario Vello (2016).

TRANSLATOR

Bhikkhu Abhinando was born in Hamburg in 1966. He became a Buddhist monk in the Theravada lineage at Chithurst Buddhist Monastery in 1994. He currently lives at Dhammapala Monastery in Switzerland. He has published three collections of poetry.

***

Dare una svolta alla parola morte
una scossa di risveglio,
farla uscire dai gusci di spavento
dei secoli e degli antenati,
farla neonata
smettere di capirla
dichiararsi incapaci
e tenerla tra le mani giunte
delicatamente
come fiammifero
nel vento.

***

To give the word death a twist,
an awakening jolt,
to set it free from the shells of fear
of centuries and ancestors,
let it be newborn,
stop understanding it,
declare oneself incapable
and hold it in joined hands
gently
like a match
in the wind

Translation by Bhikkhu Abhinando

***

Nell'orto c'è paura c'è
mezzogiorno di fuoco,
tu Bea porta con te
la tana tenera
dell'amicizia, dicono
che ho troppi doni nelle mani
e tu che nel troppo
avevi dimora, distribuiscili
tra i passeri, i lombrichi,
le chiocciole, dalli in pasto
ai trifogli e alla salvia,
non far crescere fiori
che mi rapinano lo sguardo.
Dicono che io sono sempre
in allarme, all'erta
e tu profuga smarrita
in ogni agio
spiegaglielo che sono in veglia
in canto insonne di uccelli
per ubriacatura di primavera.
Se ti portassi qui
saresti in breve la monaca folle
sposata con le piante
e gli animali e tutto il resto
che fa capolino
dal mistero.
Ci sei e non ci sei,
sei il luogo,
troppo vasta
per vederti.
Sfiorami dunque
col pensiero
come fanno le mosche
quando rincorrendosi
formano geometrie
innamorate.

***

In the garden there is fear, there is
high noon on fire,
you, Bea, take with you
the gentle cave
of friendship, they say
I have too many gifts on my hands,
and you who were at home
in the too many, share them out
between the sparrows, the worms,
the snails, give them
to the trefoil and the sage,
don't grow flowers
that will steal my sight.
They say I am always
alarmed, on alert,
and you, refugee lost
in any comfort,
explain to them that I keep vigil
with the sleepless song of birds,
drunk on spring.
If I brought you here
you would soon be the mad nun
married to the plants
and the animals and everything else
that peeps in
on the mystery.
You are here, and you are not,
you are the place,
too vast
to be seen.
Touch me then
with a thought
like the flies do
when, chasing each other,
they form geometries
in love.

Translation by Bhikkhu Abhinando

***

Vorrei guardare il mondo
con occhi di nonna,
perle svagate e tenere,
accarezzarlo
come un vecchio malato
respirare
la sua aria di pestilenza
come odori notturni di bambino.
Non temo
le sue malattie
ma i suoi gioielli acuminati
non le sue polveri sottili
ma la distanza
della guerra candida.

Mi manca
il mondo,
come una veste di pioggia
sopra la pelle graffiata
di scolara
un cielo che sillabi piano.

I momenti seduti
con te
sono strappati
al sogno operaio del mondo,
le frecce abbandonate
sul pavimento
preghiamo
di avere memoria
e sguardi senza orizzonte,
puntati,
qui.

***

I would like to look at the world
with grandmother eyes,
tender and distracted pearls,
to caress it
like a sick old man,
to breathe
its air of pestilence
like night-time smells of children.
I do not fear
its sicknesses,
but its sharpened jewels,
not its fine dust,
but the distance
of the candid war.

I miss
the world,
like a dress of rain
on the scratched skin
of a schoolgirl,
a sky that whistles quietly.

The times I sit
with you
are wrested
from the dream that fabricates the world,
the arrows left
on the pavement,
we pray
to have memory
and sight without horizon,
pointed,
here.

Di guerrieri indifesi
ha bisogno il mondo,
di sacra ira
di occhi spalancati
a bere
le sue diecimila facce
di bambino di sangue
e parola.

Cosa si dice
quando si dice
mondo
palla
che ingoia
o sbriciola
palla al piede

o quadrato ardente
di significati
rete?

Resta a terra
con il fuoco e il vento,
la farina,
e il fumo dei morti,
ogni oggetto del mondo
li contiene uno per uno
i suoi fratelli:
liberali tutti!

The world needs
helpless warriors,
holy rage,
wide-open eyes
to drink
its ten thousand faces
of a child of blood
and word.

What does one say
when one says
world,
stone
that swallows
or crumbles
stone chained to your leg

or burning square,
web of meaning?

Stay on the ground
with the fire and the wind,
the flour
and the smoke of the dead,
every object of the world
contains them one by one,
its brothers:
free them all!

Translated by Bhikkhu Abhinando

***

Ora sei trasfigurata
tutta
ora sei mondo
non mi accompagni
cammino in te
mi hai pienamente
abbandonato
riconsegnato all'intero
che sei che siamo
che mi bisbiglia notturni
e desorientando orienta
al senza meta
al silenzio.
Tu l'hai aperto
il sacco opaco il velo
l'hai divelto tu splendi.
Seduti in riva alle lacrime
pesa un quintale
la necessità di grazia.

***

Now you are transfigured
all of you,
now you are world,
you don't walk with me,
I walk inside you,
you have completely
abandoned me,
redelivered me to the whole
that you are, that we are,
that whispers nocturnes to me,
and, disorienting, orients
towards the aimless,
towards silence.
You have opened it,
the dull bag, the veil
you have torn out, you shine.
Sitting on the shore of tears,
the need for grace
weighs a ton.

Translated by Bhikkhu Abhinando

***

Amo il bianco tra le parole,
il loro margine ardente,
amo quando taci
e quando riprendi a parlare,
amo la parola che galleggia
solitaria
sullo specchio buio del vocabolario,
e quando sborda, va alla deriva
con deciso smarrimento,
quando si oscura
e quando si spezza,
si fa ombra.
Quando veste il mondo,
quando lo rivela,
quando fa mappa,
quando fa destino.
Amo quando è imminente
e quando si schianta,
quando è straniera,
quando straniera sono io
nella sua ipotetica terra,
amo quello che resta,
dopo la parola detta,
non detta. E quando è proibita
e pronunciata lo stesso,
quando si cerca e si vela,
quando si sposa
e quando è realtà dei muri
e quando sfracellarsi al suolo,
quando scorre candida
e corre per prima a bere,
e quando preme alla gola,
spinge all'aperto,
quando è presa a prestito,

***

I love the white spaces between the words,
their burning margins,
I love it when you are silent,
and when you start to talk again,
I love the word that floats
in solitude
on the dark mirror of the vocabulary,
when it overflows, when it drifts
away with decisive abandon,
when it darkens
and when it breaks,
turns into a shadow.
When it dresses the world,
when it reveals the world,
when it makes a map,
when it creates destiny.
I love it when it is imminent
and when it bursts,
when it is a stranger,
when the stranger is me
on its hypothetical earth,
I love what remains
after the spoken,
the unspoken word. And when
it is forbidden and still
pronounced,
when it searches and hides itself,
when it gets married
and when it is the reality of walls,
when it shatters on the floor,
when it walks about innocently,
and runs to drink first,
when it is stuck in the throat
and pushes out into the open,

quando mi impresta al discorso
dell'altro, quando mi abbandona.
Non voglio una parola di troppo,
voglio un silenzio a dirotto,
non un commercio tra mutezza e voce,
ma una breccia,
una ferita che allarga luce,
un sottosuolo della musica.
Dammi un amore che precipita –
parola.

when it is borrowed,
and when it lends me to the speech
of another, when it abandons me.
I don't want one word too many,
I want a hefty silence,
not some commerce between
voice and muteness,
but a breach,
a wound that gives out light,
a subsoil of music.
Give me a love that precipitates –
word.

Translated by Bhikkhu Abhinando

MILO DE ANGELIS

Milo De Angelis was born in Milan in 1951, where he currently lives as a poet, translator, teacher and literary critic. He is the author of several collections of poetry, a narrative text, many translations from the French and Greek, and a collection of essays. He is the founding editor of the magazine *Il Niebo*.

De Angelis' poetry is metropolitan, mostly set in contemporary Milan with its dilapidated yet beautiful post-industrial scenery. It is a modern form of lyricism where illness, loss and death (his wife, also a poet, died of cancer in 2003) are recurrent themes.

His poetry books are: *Somiglianze* (Guanda, 1976); *Millimetri* (Einaudi, 1983); *Terra del viso* (Mondadori, 1985); *Distante un padre* (Mondadori, 1989); *Biografia sommaria* (Mondadori, 1999); *Tema dell'addio* (Mondadori, 2005); *Quell'andare andare nel buio dei cortili* (Mondadori, 2010); and *Incontri e agguati* (Mondadori, 2015). In 1915, the publishing house Mondadori printed the complete collection of his verses *Tutte le poesie* 1969–2015. In 2017, he published a book of interviews with Mimesis, *La parola data*, with a DVD by Viviana Nicodemo. His latest collection is *Linea intera, linea spezzata*, (Mondadori, 2021).

De Angelis has also written the novella *La corsa dei mantelli* (Guanda, 1979) and a volume of essays, *Poesia e destino* (Cappelli, 1982).

TRANSLATORS

Patrizio Ceccagnoli is an Associate Professor of Italian at the University of Kansas. In collaboration with Susan Stewart, Ceccagnoli translated two books of Milo de Angelis' poetry, *Theme of Farewell and After-Poems* (2013). This volume was nominated for the American Literary Translator's Association Annual Award in 2014.

Susan Stewart is an American poet and literary critic. She is the Avalon Foundation University Professor in the Humanities and Professor of English at Princeton University. Her most recent books are *Cinder: New and Selected Poems* and *The Ruins Lesson: Meaning and Material in Western Culture*. Her co-translation, with Patrizio Ceccagnoli, of Antonella Anedda's *Historiae* will be out in 2022.

***

Milano era asfalto, asfalto liquefatto. Nel deserto
di un giardino avvenne la carezza, la penombra
addolcita che invase le foglie, ora senza giudizio,
spazio assoluto di una lacrima. Un istante
in equilibrio tra due nomi avanzò verso di noi,
si fece luminoso, si posò respirando sul petto,
sulla grande presenza sconosciuta. Morire fu quello
sbriciolarsi delle linee, noi lì e il gesto ovunque,
noi dispersi nelle supreme tensioni dell'estate,
noi tra le ossa e l'essenza della terra.

***

Milan was asphalt, liquid asphalt. In the desert
of a garden there was a caress, the melting
penumbra invading the leaves, the hour without censure,
a tear's absolute space. An instant
balanced between two names came toward us
luminous, breathing, and settling on the chest,
on the great unknown presence. To die was that
crumbling of lines, we were there and the gesture was everywhere,
we were scattered in the high tensions of summer,
we were caught between the bones and the essence of the earth.

Translation by Patrizio Ceccagnoli and Susan Stewart

***

Non è più dato. Il pianto che si trasformava
in un ridere impazzito, le notti passate
correndo in Via Crescenzago, inseguendo il neon
di un'edicola. Non è più dato. Non è più nostro
il batticuore di aspettare mezzanotte, aspettarla
finché mezzanotte entra nel suo vero tumulto,
nella frenesia di tutte le ore, di tutte le ore.
Non è più dato. Uno solo è il tempo, una sola
la morte, poche le ossessioni, poche
le notti d'amore, pochi i baci, poche le strade
che portano fuori di noi, poche le poesie.

***

It's no longer possible. The crying that turned
into crazy laughing, the nights spent
running down Via Crescenzago, chasing the neon
banner of a newsstand. It's no longer possible. It's no longer ours,
the heartbeat of waiting for midnight, waiting for her
until midnight enters with its true tumult,
with the frenzy of all the hours, all the hours.
It's no longer possible. There's only one time, only one
death, a few obsessions, a few
nights of love, a few kisses, a few streets
that lead outside ourselves, a few poems.

Translation by Patrizio Ceccagnoli and Susan Stewart

***

Tutto era già in cammino. Da allora a qui. Tutto
il tempo, luminoso, sfiorava le labbra. Tutti
i respiri si riunivano nella collana. Le ombre
di Lambrate chiusero la porta. Tutta la stanza,
assorta, diventò il primo battito. Il nero
dei tuoi capelli contro il giallo dell'ultimo raggio.
Da allora a qui. Era il primo giorno dell'estate.
Il silenzio ci riempiva la fronte. Tutto era
già in cammino, da allora, tutto era qui, unico
e perduto, nostro e remoto, ardente. Tutto chiedeva
di essere atteso, di tornare nel suo vero nome.

***

Everything was already on its way. From then to here. All
of time, luminous, skimmed across the lips. All
the sighs strung on the necklace. Lambrate's
shadows shut the door. The whole room,
taken in, became the first heartbeat. The black
of your hair against the yellow of the last sunbeams.
From then to here. It was the first day of summer.
Silence filled our thoughts. Everything was
already on its way, from then on, everything was here, unique
and lost, ours and far from us, burning. Everything asked
us to wait for it, to return to its true name.

Translation by Patrizio Ceccagnoli and Susan Stewart

***

Non c'era più tempo. La camera era entrata in una fiala.
Non era più dato spartire l'essenza. Non avevi
più la collana. Non avevi più tempo. Il tempo era una luce
marina tra le persiane, una festa di sorelle,
la ferita, l'acqua alla gola, Villa Litta. Non c'era
più giorno. L'ombra della terra riempiva gli occhi
con la paura dei colori scomparsi. Ogni molecola
era in attesa. Abbiamo guardato il rammendo
delle mani. Non c'era più luce. Ancora una volta
ci stanno chiamando, giudicati da una stella fissa.

***

There was no more time. The room was poured into a phial.
It was no longer possible to share the essence. You no longer had
the necklace. You were out of time. Time was a light
from the sea, through the shutters, a party of sisters,
the wound, the water at the throat, Villa Litta. There was no
more day. The earth's shadow was brimming our eyes
with the fear of vanished colours. Every molecule
was waiting. We looked at the hands'
mending. There was no more light. Once again
they call us, judged by a fixed star.

Translation by Patrizio Ceccagnoli and Susan Stewart

***

Il luogo era immobile, la parola scura. Era quello
il luogo stabilito. Addio memoria di notti
lucenti, addio grande sorriso. Il luogo era lì.
Respirare fu un buio di persiane, uno stare primitivo.
Silenzio e deserto si scambiavano volto e noi
parlavamo a una lampada. Il luogo era quello. I tram
passavano radi. Venere ritornava nella sua baracca.
Dalla gola guerriera si staccavano episodi. Non abbiamo
detto più niente. Il luogo era quello. Era lì
che stavi morendo.

***

The place was motionless, the word obscure. That was
the place we settled on. Goodbye, memory of the sparkling
nights, goodbye, big smile. The place was there.
To breathe was a darkness shutters had made, a primitive state.
Silence and desert were switching looks and we
were talking to a lamp. The place was that one. The trolleys
rarely passed. Venus was returning to her hut.
Out of the warrior throat, episodes broke free. We didn't
say anything more. The place was that one. It was there
that you were dying.

Translation by Patrizio Ceccagnoli and Susan Stewart

MATTEO FANTUZZI

Matteo Fantuzzi was born in 1979 in Bologna, and lives in Lugo di Romagna, near Ravenna. He has published two poetry collections: *Kobarid* (Raffaelli, 2008) and *La stazione di Bologna* (Feltrinelli, 2017).

Fantuzzi's poetry explores the repressed memories of contemporary Italy and its inability to cope (culturally and politically) with the re-emergence of Fascism. His poems have appeared in many magazines. Fantuzzi is a co-director of *Mosaics* magazine at St. Andrews University in Scotland, editor of *Atelier* magazine and the director of the contemporary poetry series of Ladolfi Editore. The creator of the portal UniversoPoesia, he has also edited the anthologies *La linea del Sillaro sulla Poesia dell'Emilia-Romagna* (Campanotto, 2006); *La generazione entrante sui poeti nati negli anni Ottanta* (Ladolfi, 2011); and, together with Isabella Leardini, *Post '900. Lyrics and narratives* (Landolfi, 2014). He is a digital writer for *l'Unità*.

TRANSLATOR

Lara Ferrini works as a high school English teacher in Morciano di Romagna. She has a PhD in European Cultural Studies. She has published essays about Irish contemporary poets (Desmond Egan, Pat Boran, and Medbh McGuckian) and translated a selection of their work into Italian.

Il senso di una strage

C'è un attimo avvenuta
l'esplosione, tra le macerie
e i vetri, in cui si quieta tutto

prima delle grida, delle sirene
concitate: è un attimo
nel quale non si crede veramente
che sia accaduto quello che si vede.

È lì che si comprende
il senso di una strage,
quando il silenzio avvolge e copre
senza scelta e senza distinzione

come la gente attorno a una stazione
che prende il treno per lavoro
o per le ferie, a inizio agosto
di mattina, come sempre.

The meaning of a massacre

There's an instant when
the explosion is over, among the ruins
and the glass, when everything calms down

before the shouting, the sirens
agitated: it's an instant
when we don't really believe
what we saw has happened.

That's when we understand
the meaning of a massacre,
when the silence wraps and covers itself
without choice and without distinction

like the people at a station
who catch a train for work
or for holidays, at the beginning of August
in the morning, like usual.

Translation by Lara Ferrini

Come un padre che scava solo e a mani nude

nei giorni successivi i taxi sono gratis per i parenti
delle vittime ricoverate presso gli ospedali cittadini.

Come un padre che scava solo e a mani nude
un figlio fino a sanguinare e che non smette
se lo getta addosso e non lo lascia,
carne della carne, pure se una gamba resta
sotto le macerie e Marco non potrà più essere
mezz'ala e correre veloce sotto la tribuna,
oppure tra i distinti laterali proprio dove stanno
spesso i familiari che applaudono comunque
qualsiasi cosa accada, perfino dopo una sconfitta:
come fa chi aspetta a casa con il fuoco caldo
sotto la minestra e che comunque resta.

Like a father who digs alone for his son with bare hands

in the following days taxis were free for the relatives
of the victims admitted to the town hospitals

Like a father who digs alone for his son with bare hands
until bleeding and who doesn't stop
he pulls him on to himself and doesn't leave him,
his own flesh and blood, even if a leg remains
under the ruins and Marco won't be
an outside midfielder anymore and won't run fast in front of the tribune,
or among the side tribunes just where the relatives
often sit clapping anyway
whatever happens, even after a defeat:
as does the one that waits at home with the warm fire
some soup and that in any case remains.

Translation by Lara Ferrini

Se dalla Piazza ti incammini e prendi i portici

scoppia una bomba
nel cuore di Bologna.
due agosto ottanta.

Se dalla Piazza ti incammini e prendi i portici
del centro e riesci a superare in un sol colpo
quella folla, i saldi, le vetrine, i tavolini delle firme,
se riesci a non fermarti davanti a quel barbone
inginocchiato a mo' di Cristo che chiede
le monete e prega tutti per i soldi, se a un tratto
ti fai forza e inizi a correre smettendo di vedere
altrove ti troverai d'un tratto alla sinistra
il luogo steso a gambe aperte e in mezzo la ferita
che ancora accenna, che ricorda il giorno
in cui la gente è stata tutta uguale per una volta,
                              e solo quella.
Tutti comunisti, preti. Tutti bolognesi.

If from the Square you start walking and stay under the arches

A bomb exploded
in the heart of Bologna
Second of August 1980

If from the Square you start walking and stay under the arches
in the city centre and manage to pass it in one fell swoop
that crowd, the sales, the shop windows, the small desks for signatures,
if you manage not to stop in front of that homeless
on his knees as a Christ who is begging for
coins, and who is praying to everybody for money, if all of a sudden
you remain strong and start running stopping to glance
elsewhere you will find yourself all of a sudden on the left
the place lying with open legs and in the middle the wound
which still gives a hint, which remembers the day
when people were the same for that one time,
                              and only that one.
All communists, priests. All *bolognesi.*

Translation by Lara Ferrini

Crollano le travi, cadono le pietre e i calcinacci

L'esplosione della stazione coinvolge non solo le strutture della sala d'attesa ma anche i sovrastanti uffici amministrativi della Cigar. Euridia, Katia, Nilla, Rita, Franca e Mirella muoiono nel crollo della struttura.

Crollano le travi, cadono le pietre e i calcinacci,
vola via l'età dell'innocenza ormai tradita
dalle cose, qui tutto è ricordo: ogni palazzo,
strada, parco, ogni momento ha una sua storia
che preme e urge come l'esigenza di memoria.
Di qua c'è un corpo immobile che cerca
ossigeno tra i cocci, alla sua destra
si intravede appena un piede senza scarpa,
un uomo grida e cerca la sorella, un altro
piange. Un padre copre con il corpo i figli,
li abbraccia come alla mattina si proteggono
dagli incubi, dai mostri che in fondo al sonno
vengono e devastano.

È quotidiana questa strategia
della tensione, non abbandona mai davvero.

Collapsing crossbeams, falling stones and rubble

The explosion of the railway station involved not only the structures of the waiting room, but also the overlying administrative offices of the Cigar. Euridia, Katia, Nilla, Rita, Franca and Mirella died in the collapse of the structure.

Collapsing crossbeams, falling stones and rubble
flying away the age of innocence by now cheated on
by things, here everything is a memory: every building,
road, park, every moment has its own history
which pushes and it's urgent like the need for remembrance.
Here is a still body which is looking for
oxygen among the shards, on its right-hand side
a foot without a shoe barely seen,
a man is shouting and looking for his sister, another one
is crying. A father is covering his children with his body,
he's hugging them like in the morning they are protected
from their nightmares, from the monsters that deep in sleep
come and devastate.

It's daily this strategy
of tension, it never really gives up.

Translation by Lara Ferrini

Adesso questi volti sono tutti familiari

Adesso questi volti sono tutti familiari
li rivedo ovunque, sono i miei clienti del lavoro
o le cassiere del supermercato, o i ragazzini
delle scuole, i pensionati che divorano i giornali
nei lunghi viali della biblioteca. Vedo Torquato
e Carlo, Silvana e Mirco, Nazzareno, Salvatore
che hanno la mia età e un poco mi somigliano
rivedo Angela – 3 anni – che mi corre incontro
come Federico adesso, solo con il volto di Sofia,
che ancora non conosco. Poi Vincenzo che esce
dalle porte delle case qui a Bagnacavallo
e se ne va a Verona per vedere l'opera, anche lui
lo vedo tutti i giorni, è nei teatri in terza fila
sulla destra: non si perde neanche un attimo la scena
conosce ogni passaggio (io invece mi addormento
a volte, mi metto a scrivere, mi perdo). Ci sono
certi giorni che mi vengono a trovare tutti,
mi raccontano talmente tante cose che non riesco
neanche a contenerle. Allora sfuggono e ritornano
come fa la neve che si deposita poi ghiaccia
pazienta e quando esplode infine bagna
i campi e porta frutto, e non ti lascia.

Angela Fresu, figlia di Maria di cui non ritrovarono mai il corpo, solo alcuni resti saldati alle macerie dopo molti mesi, troppo vicina al punto d'esplosione perché non rimanesse altro che il ricordo.

Now these faces are all familiar

Now these faces are all familiar
I see them again everywhere, they are my clients at work
or the supermarket check-out girls, or the little
school boys, the pensioners devouring newspapers
in the long boulevards of the library. I see Torquato
and Carlo, Silvana and Mirco, Nazzareno, Salvatore
who are the same age as me and they look like me a bit
I see Angela again – 3 years old – who is running towards me
like Federico now, alone with Sofia's face,
whom I don't know yet. Then Vincenzo who comes out
from the doors of the houses here in Bagnacavallo
and goes to Verona to attend the opera, even him
I see him every day, he's in the theatres in the third row
on the right: not for a moment does he miss the scene
he knows every single line (I fall asleep instead
sometimes, I start writing, I get lost). There are
some days when everybody comes to visit me,
they tell me such a lot of things that I can't
even keep them in. Then they run away and come back
like the patient snow that settles then turns
into ice and when it blows up in the end it wets
the fields and bears fruit, and it doesn't leave you.

Angela Fresu, Maria's daughter, whose corpse was never found, just some remains under the ruins after many months. She was so close to the blast point that just the memory remained.

Translation by Lara Ferrini

SHIRIN RAMZANALI FAZEL

Shirin Ramzanali Fazel (Mogadishu,1953) is an Italian author of Somali and Pakistani origins. Her lyrical memoir, *Lontano da Mogadiscio* (1994), is considered a milestone of Italian postcolonial literature. Fazel's novel, *Nuvole sull'Equatore* (2010), is about a young woman of mixed race growing up during the Italian Trusteeship Administration of Somalia. Both her books were reworked and self-translated into English.

In 2018, Fazel self-published *Wings*, her first poetry collection in English; later self-translated and published in Italian with the title *Ali Spezzate*. She was a member of the Advisory Board of Transnationalizing Modern Languages, a project funded by the Arts and Humanity Research Council. She has also led, in collaboration with the universities of Cardiff, Warwick and Namibia, a series of creative writing workshops and published several short stories and poems in anthologies and magazines. Fazel is an active member of Writers Without Borders based in Birmingham. Her latest book, co-authored with Simone Brioni, is *Scrivere di Islam. Raccontare la Diaspora* (Cà Foscari University Press, 2021).

Love letter to my hometown
Kuala Lumpur: January 20, 2017

Assalamu' Alaikum Wa Rahmatuullahi Wa Barakatuh
May Peace and Mercy and the Blessings of Allah be upon you

My beloved Xamar,

Yours was the first air I breathed
The first blue sky my eyes gazed on
I daydreamed watching your white and pink clouds

hooyo – mother you nourished me
Our lively ancient neighbourhood protected me
Abti – Uncle, *habaryar* – auntie and *ayeeyo* – grandmother
None of them tied to me by blood
Made me feel I belonged to a large noisy *reer* – family

I treasure
The voices, the scent and the taste of Boondheere,
Via Roma, Shingaani, Xamar Weyne and the Tamarind market

In exile on lonely nights
I have longed for
Your warm salty ocean waves
And the slightly fermented taste of *caano geel* – camel milk

I wept bitter tears
When I saw you bleeding
And my large noisy family
Wounded, maimed, killed

Mogadishu
Like a lost child I dream of you
My heart will never fall in love again

Lettera d'amore alla mia città natale
Kuala Lumpur, 20 Gennaio 2017

Assalamu' Alaikum Wa Rahmatuullahi Wa Barakatuh
Che la pace e la misericordia di Allah sia su di te

Mia amata Xamar

La tua è stata la prima aria che ho respirato
Il primo cielo azzurro che il mio sguardo ha fissato
Ho sognato ad occhi aperti guardando le tue nuvole bianche e rosa

Come *hooyo* una madre tu mi hai allevata
I tuoi antichi quartieri mi hanno protetto
Abti zii, *habaryar* zie e *ayeeyo* nonne
Nessuno dei quali parenti di sangue
Mi hanno fatto sentire di appartenere ad una grande famiglia chiassosa

Io amo
Le voci, i profumi e i sapori di Boondheere,
Via Roma, Shingaani, Xamar Weyne e il mercato del Tamarindo

In esilio nelle notti solitarie
Ho bramato
Le calde onde del tuo oceano salato
E il gusto agro di *caano geel* latte di cammella

Ho pianto lacrime amare
Quando ti ho vista sanguinare
E la mia famiglia chiassosa
Ferita, mutilata, uccisa

Mogadiscio
Come una bambina sperduta io sogno te
Il mio cuore non s'innamorerà mai di nuovo

You only you
Can make me cry, laugh,
Bring back memories of my childhood
The pain of the present
And hope for a better future

We belong to each other,
My beloved Xamar

Shirin Ramzanali Fazel

Tu e solo tu
Puoi farmi piangere e ridere
Fai rifiorire i miei ricordi dell'infanzia
Il dolore del presente
E la speranza per un futuro migliore

Noi ci apparteniamo
Mia amata Xamar

Shirin Ramzanali Fazel

Afka hooyo – Mother Tongue

The sounds I carry in my memories:
I live in this bubble of voices –
The sweet warm milk suckled from *hooyo*'s generous breast,
My falling into sleep covered in a blanket of words…

My first steps: I wobble, I fall, salty tears ploughing down my face…
I look at the blue sky,
I stutter, struggle – a funny sound…
Hooyo laughs – she giggles…
She makes me repeat the same word again and again.
Her eyes flicker like the first stars that peep in the inky night.

The sound of this language has memories
Built brick by brick,
It can move my deepest emotions –
The hidden ones
Like pearls buried at the bottom of the sea.
This language is not always
Mellow, pure, soft, musical, kind –
This same language
Can hurt, curse, wound my heart and leave invisible scars:
These guttural harsh sounds can heal my soul.

I carry these notes like a timeless instrument:
I am the howling sound of the arid desert wind,
The pungent scent of the bush,
The early raindrops of *Gu* and *Dayr* – spring and autumn,
I am the music of camel bells marching towards abundance,
I am the cracking sound of charcoal burning *lubaan* – frankincense,
I am the frail sobbing of a moaning tribe,
Of a child crying for help…
I am the ruthless echo of uninvited bullets,
Of hatred and destruction,
I am the bitter soul whispering prayers…

Afka hooyo – Lingua madre

Conservo suoni nella mia memoria
Io vivo in quella bolla di voci
Il dolce latte materno poppato dal generoso seno di *hooyo*
Sprofondo nel sonno sotto ad una coperta di parole...

I miei primi passi: barcollo, cado, lacrime salate mi rigano il viso...
Guardo il cielo azzurro,
Balbetto, mi sforzo – un suono buffo...
Hooyo ride una risata allegra...
Mi fa ripetere la stessa parola di nuovo e ancora di nuovo.
I suoi occhi brillano come la prima stella che sbircia nella notte scura.

Il suono di questa lingua ha una memoria
Costruita mattone per mattone,
Può scatenare le mie emozioni profonde
Quelle nascoste
Come perle sepolte nella profondità del mare.
Questa lingua non è sempre
Suadente, pura, musicale, generosa, calma
Questa stessa lingua
Può offendere, maledire, ferire il mio cuore lasciando cicatrici invisibili
Questi suoni penetranti, gutturali possono sanare la mia anima

Come uno strumento senza tempo io mi porto dietro queste note
Il vento ululante dell'arido deserto e
Il profumo pungente della boscaglia
Le prime gocce di pioggia del *Gu* primavera e di *Dayr* autunno
Il tintinnio dei campanelli di legno che i cammelli portano al
collo mentre marciano verso l'abbondanza,
Lo schiocco del carbone ardente mentre brucia *lubaan* incenso
Il debole singhiozzo di una tribù in lutto,
Di un bambino che chiede aiuto contro odio e distruzione.
È l'anima triste che mormora preghiere

I struggle when I have to read this language I love most,
Written in an alphabet adopted from a foreign land,
Signs not strong enough to lift my heavy tongue –
I feel like a ballerina dancing on a broken toe.
I abandon this newspaper,
I refuse to read these words:
Burcad badeed, burbur, baahi, argagixiso, cadow –
Pirates, destruction, poverty, terrorism, enemy…
Dagaal, dhimasho, dhiig –
War, death, blood…

I treasure the language of poets:
Hooyo's lullabies,
Jokes and proverbs…
Blessings and goodness –
Barako iyo wanaag

Io fatico quando devo leggere il linguaggio che amo tanto
Scritto in un alfabeto adottato da una terra straniera
Segni deboli che non riescono a muovere la mia pesante lingua
Mi sento come una ballerina con l'alluce rotto,
Io scaravento
Mi rifiuto di leggere
Burcad badeed, burbur, baahi, argagixiso, cadow
Pirati, distruzione, povertà, terrorismo, nemici…
Dagal, dhimasho, dhiig
Guerra, morte, sangue…

Io amo la poesia
La ninna nanna di *hooyo*
I proverbi e le barzellette
Le benedizioni e la gentilezza
Barako iyo wanaag

Translation by the author

Stubbornness

I got into trouble in school
My small arms knotted around my waist
I sweat trying to translate
The teacher's words

Mother you are not familiar
With this foreign language

Mother your round dark face
Watching me
Your piercing pitch-dark eyes
Reading my thoughts
Like a simple book

    I lower my gaze
    I am too proud to lie

Your guttural voice
Gets muffled
Your inquisitive eyes become slits
You clench your fists
Bite your upper lip

    My tongue is like a contortionist
    Twisting rolling pulling
    That magic muscle

I look at the teacher
Her mouth like a whistling kettle
Words flow

Ostinazione

Mi sono messo nei guai a scuola
Ho le braccia intorno alla vita
Sto sudando
Cerco di tradurre
Le parole della maestra

Mamma non ti è familiare
Questa lingua straniera

Mamma il tuo volto rotondo e scuro
Fisso su di me
I tuoi occhi penetranti
Leggono i miei pensieri
Come un semplice libro

      Abbasso lo sguardo
      Sono troppo orgoglioso per mentire

La tua voce rauca
È smorzata
I tuoi occhi inquisitori diventano due lame
Stringi i pugni
Mordi il tuo labbro superiore

      La mia lingua è come una contorsionista
      Ruota avvolge tira
      Quel muscolo magico

Io guardo la maestra
La sua bocca è come
Un bollitore fischiettante
Frasi che sgorgano

I try to translate
But the words are too long
I waver can't find a good match
My mind is wandering

I swallow the words
Stuck in my throat
My tummy groans
I hold my bladder

Sunshine is knocking boldly on the window
I hear the chirping voices of children playing
I imagine white-grey feathered seagulls
Sleeping on the slippery roof

Cerco di tradurre
Ma le parole sono troppo lunghe
Esito non riesco a trovare le frasi giuste
La mia mente vaga

Inghiottisco le parole
Bloccate in gola
Il mio pancino brontola
Mi tengo la pipì

Il sole bussa spavaldo dalla finestra
Sento le voci dei bambini che giocano
Immagino gabbiani dalle piume bianche e grigie
Che sonnecchiano sui tetti scivolosi

Translation by the author

115

Pick and choose

Pick and choose
Like cattle
Fit for the market

Endless documents
Forms
Questionnaires
To be filled

It is your colour
That says it all

You are not good enough
You are young strong
You have brains
To become someone
If only you had the chance

You are not good enough
You want to live
You want to work
You want to have a family

You are not good enough
You are 'black'!
Go back!

Scegli e prendi

Scegli e prendi
Come mandrie
Buone per il mercato

Infinite pratiche
Moduli
Schede
Questionari
Da compilare

È il tuo colore
Che la dice tutta

Non sei buono abbastanza
Sei giovane e forte
Hai cervello
Per diventare qualcuno
Se solo tu avessi la possibilità

Non sei buono abbastanza
Tu vuoi vivere
Vuoi lavorare
Vuoi avere una famiglia

Non sei buono abbastanza
Tu sei 'nero'
Torna indietro

Translation by the author

Shambles

Endings
Come by surprise
And they can be
The worst nightmare

Your home pounded to the ground
By an enemy you have never met
The lush pomegranate tree
You planted for your son Sami Burnt out
Its branches spread Lifeless
Its red flowers
Scattered like blood

    Your loving wife Wafaa
    Your devoted mother
    Your sleek dark-haired child Hannah
    Buried under rubble

When your fingers bleed
And your heart pleads
When your tears flow dry
And your tongue is thirsty

    When pigeons don't coo
    When all the air stinks
    When kites don't fly
    And church bells don't chime

How do you begin?

Stragi

La fine
Ti coglie sempre di sorpresa
E può
Diventare il peggiore degli incubi

La tua casa ridotta in macerie
Da un nemico che non hai mai incontrato
Il rigoglioso albero di melograno
Che hai piantato per tuo figlio Sami
Bruciato
I suoi rami sparsi
Senza vita
I suoi fiori rossi
Disseminati come schizzi di sangue

    La tua adorata moglie Wafa
    La tua dolce mamma
    La tua bambina Hanna
    Dai lunghi capelli scuri
    Seppellite sotto alle macerie

Quando le tue dita sanguinano
E il tuo cuore implora
Quando piangi senza lacrime
E la tua gola
È arsa dalla sete

    Quando i piccioni non tubano
    E l'aria intorno a te è nauseante
    Quando gli aquiloni non volano
    E le campane delle chiese non suonano

Come farai a ricominciare?

                Translation by the author

FABIO FRANZIN

Fabio Franzin was born in Milan in 1963 and lives in Motta di Livenza, near Treviso. A factory worker since the age of sixteen, Franzin reflects on the loss of identity and aspirations of the working classes, now de-unionised, fragmented and dispersed by neoliberal policies and globalisation.

His poems are mostly written in the dialect of Veneto-Treviso. The marginalised become the dissident voices of a society that has betrayed their people. Franzin has published several poetry collections including: *El coeor dee paròe* (Zone, 2000); *Canzón daa Provenza (e altre trazhe d'amór)* (Fondazione Corrente, 2005); *Pare* (Helvetia, 2006); *Mus.cio e roe* (Le voci della luna, 2007); *Fabrica* (Atelier, 2009); *Rosario de siénzhi* (trilingual edition: Italian, Slovenian and Veneto, Postaja Topolove, 2010); *Siénzhio e orazhión* (Edizioni Prioritarie, 2010); *Co'e man monche* (Le voci della luna, 2011); *Sesti / Gesti (Puntoacapo Editrice, 2015)*; *Corpo dea realtà* (Culturaglobale, 2016 and 2019); *Erba e aria* (Vydia editore, 2017); *'A fabrica ribandonàdha* (Arcipelago itaca Edizioni, 2021). Franzin's poems have been translated into English, French, Chinese, Arabic, German, Spanish, Catalan and Slovenian.

TRANSLATOR

Cristina Viti is a translator and poet working with Italian, English and French. Recent translations include Anna Gréki's *The Streets of Algiers* (Smokestack Books, 2020); Mariangela Gualtieri's *Beast of Joy* (Chelsea Editions, 2018), and Elsa Morante's *The World Saved by Kids* (Seagull Books, 2016), shortlisted for the John Florio Prize.

***

Marta l'à quarantatrè àni.
Da vintizhinque 'a grata
cornìse co'a carta de véro,
el tanpón, 'a ghe russa via
'a vernìse dura dae curve

del 'egno; e ghe 'à restà
come un segno tee man:
carézhe che sgrafa, e onge
curte, da òn. I só bèi cavéi
biondi e bocoeósi i 'é 'dèss

un grop de spaghi stopósi
che nissùna peruchièra pòl
pì tornàr rizhàr. Co'a cata
'e só care amighe maestre
o segretarie, ghe par che

'e sie tant pì zóvene de ea,
'a ghe invidia chee onge
cussì rosse e longhe, i cavéi
lissi e luminosi, chii déi
ben curàdhi, co' i sii pàra

drio 'e rece, i recìni. Le
varda e spess 'a pensa
al só destìn: tuta 'na vita
persa a gratàr, a gratarse
via dal corpo 'a beézha.

122

***

Marta is forty-three.
Twenty-five spent rubbing
frames smooth with sandpaper &
block, buffing the hard
varnish off the moulded

edges of wood. And that has left
a sort of mark on her hands
a scratch in the stroking, nails
short, like a man's. Her lovely hair
from fair & curly down to

a knot of coarse twine
no stylist can ever
curl back into shape. When she meets
her good friends who are
teachers or secretaries, she thinks

they look so much younger than her,
looks in envy at those well-buffed
long red nails, at their smooth
glossy hair, well-groomed
fingers that adjust it

behind their ears, at the earrings. She
looks at them & often thinks
of her fate: all her life
wasted in rubbing, rubbing her
body bare of its charm.

Translation by Cristina Viti

Me despiase

Ieri, el kosovaro che 'l lavora co' mì
el me 'à domandà se podhée prestarghe
zhinquanta euro, el se vardéa tii pie

pa' far su 'l coràjo de chee paròe
chissà par quant rumegàdhe – lo sa
che 'ò dó fiòi, el mutuo pa'a casa

e tut el resto – e za 'l savéa, son sicuro
anca 'a mé risposta, parché no'l se 'à
ciapàdha, sì, sì, certo, capisco l'à dita

sgorlàndo 'a testa intànt che 'ndessi
verso i reparti, i guanti strenti tea man.
Però mi nò che no' lo riconossée pì

co'là che ghe 'à tocà dir mi dispiace
proprio co' ièra drio sonàr 'a sirena
e no' restéa tenpo nianca pa'a vergogna.

Sorry

Yesterday, my Kosovar workmate
asked me could I lend him
fifty euros – looking down at his feet

working up courage to say those words
mulled over who knows how long –
he knows I've two kids & the mortgage

& all the rest – & for sure also knew
my answer already, 'cause he didn't
get mad, yes, yes he said, I understand

shaking his head as we made our way
to the shop floor, clutching our gloves.
But me, I could not recognise the other guy

the one who found himself having to say sorry
just as the siren started off
with not even any time left for shame.

Translation by Cristina Viti

Artù

El scavo l'é quel pa'e fondamenta,
un buso grando, largo, scuro; in banda
'na mùtera de tèra smossa come quea
che buta su 'e rùmoe tel prà. Lo varde

in fra un sbrègo del teo aranción tut
a busi del rezhinto, te 'sti dì de vent
e gèo. Tea mùtera dura come cròdha
calche murèr l'à piantà là un badhìl.

No'é pì tenpi de fàvoe e lejende, lo
so, e so che l'Artù che un dì cavarà
via el badhìl daa tèra 'l sarà albanese
o romeno, fòra règoea, pagà in nero,

e so che no'l deventarà re, dopo, che
no'l podharà portar pase e ben, salvar
un regno in crisi. Resta chel pal sbiègo
come orméjo pa' picàr i nòvi s.ciavi.

Arthur

The trench is the one dug for foundations,
a wide gash, a big dark hole; on its side
a mound of broken earth like the ones
moles make in the fields. I watch it

from a gash in the tatty orange tarp
of the fencing, in these days of gale
& freezing cold. Rock-hard mound,
& a spade stuck in there by a navvy.

I know these are not the times of yore,
& I know the Arthur who one day will pull
the spade from the soil will be Albanian,
Romanian, black economy, cash-in-hand,

I know he'll not be made king after that,
he'll not be able to bring peace & save
a kingdom in crisis. What's left is that spade
a skewed mooring to shackle new slaves.

Translation by Cristina Viti

127

***

No l'é pecà a ragàr
'na rosa dal rosèr, se
tì che te 'a spèta te 'iuta
'a sera a fiorìr de un canto.

Intanto 'e pavéjie 'e me saeùdha,
e dal fondo de l'aria mòre
el ciaro te 'a grazia de l'ort.
'Na zhiìga 'a se pudha tea paeàdha.

E mì son vestì da festa.
'Ò 'na camisa bianca come
un fòjio. La 'ò messa su parché tì
te ghe scrive sora un poema de carezhe.

***

No sin in robbing
a rose off its bush if
you who await it can bring
the evening to blossom in song.

Meanwhile its butterflies greet me,
& deep in the air light is fading
in the calmed grace of the kitchen garden.
A sparrow alights on the fence.

And I'm in my Sunday best.
Wearing a shirt that's white as
a sheet. I've put it on for you
to write on it a poem of caresses.

Translation by Cristina Viti

***

L'é drio inbrunìr.
El vent fa zhigàr i veri,
e mi magne pan e fighi
e varde fora, lavìa in fondo,
el prà che se indormenzha
senpre pì, senpre de pì,

Fra poc dovarò impizhar 'a luce
se vui, se deve veder 'a me man
che, pinpian, 'a ' me carezha.

***

It's getting dark.
Glass panes wailing in the wind
as I sit eating bread & figs
& looking outside, far outside
at the meadow falling asleep,
a little more, a little more,

Before long I'll have to turn on the light
if I want, if I must see my hand
as it strokes me slowly, so slowly.

Translation by Cristina Viti

MARCO GIOVENALE

Marco Giovenale was born in 1969 and lives in Rome, where he works as an editor and translator. He researches, writes and promotes experimental poetry both in Italian and English. He also teaches Literature at the UPTER University, where he founded and is one of the directors of the Centro di poesia e scritture contemporanee. Giovenale is also founder and editor of a number of magazines and websites: *bina* (2003), *gammm.org* (2006), *ponte bianco* (2008), *Punto critico* (2011; now blog: puntocritico2.wordpress.com), *eexxiitt* (2011), and asemicnet.blogspot.com (2011).

Giovenale's books of poetry are: *Criterio dei vetri* (Oèdipus, 2007); *La casa esposta* (Le Lettere, 2007); *Soluzione della materia* (La camera verde, 2009); *Storia dei minuti* (Transeuropa, 2010); *Shelter* (Donzelli, 2010); *In rebus* (Zona, 2012, 'Level 48' series); *Delvaux* (Oèdipus, 2013); *Maniera nera* (Aragno, 2015); and *Strettoie* (Arcipelago Itaca, 2017). His published prose works are: *Numeri primi* (Arcipelago, 2006); *Quasi tutti* (Polìmata, 2010; new edition Miraggi, 2018); *Lie lie* (La camera verde, 2010); *Phobos* (Benway sheets, 2014, French translation by M. Zaffarano); *Numeri morali* (gammm e-book, 2014); and *Il paziente crede di essere* (Gorilla Sapiens, 2016).

TRANSLATORS

Linh Dinh is a poet, fiction writer, translator and photographer. He was born in Saigon, Vietnam in 1963, moved to the US in 1975, and has also lived in Italy and England. Dinh is the recipient of a Pew Foundation Grant, the David T.K. Wong Fellowship, a Lannan residency, and the Asian American Literary Award.

Jennifer Scappettone works at the confluence of the literary, visual, and scholarly arts. Her translations of Amelia Rosselli were gathered in the award-winning collection *Locomotrix*, and she curates PennSound | Italiana. Her poetry collections include *From Dame Quickly*, *The Republic of Exit 43*, and *Belladonna Elders Series #5: Poetry, Landscape, Apocalypse* (with Etel Adnan and Lyn Hejinian). She is Associate Professor at the University of Chicago and Visiting Professor at the Université Gustave Eiffel.

***

...   riga (una: un) picco voltaico
di luce fa però perplessi ancora

pochi oggetti bianchi –
si vedono. Cialde.

Comme des larmes
scialbe. Larve.

(Chiodarle)

***

...   line (one: a) voltaic peak
of light still puzzles a

few white objects–
they can be seen. Waffles.

Comme des larmes
pale. Larvae.

(To nail them.)

Translation by Jennifer Scappettone

***

già alle sette, a luce iniziata,
il sudore alla gola

un braccio irrelato
che si smorza e rimane

filtrano i soliti due
panico, piante : e: sterri, agosto

arteria vena
un culto di ossa corte

bucate a un estremo
per: fissarle, a parete

o petto. La riga di ocra
indica l'uscita del respiro –

la consuetudine di portare
addosso resti umani

***

already at 7 o'clock, as light struck,
the sweating throat

an unconnected arm
that dims and remains

the usual two transpire :
panic, plants : and : earthworks, August

artery, vein,
a cult of short bones

with holes at one end
to: fasten them, to a wall

or chest. The ochre line
shows where breath gets out –

the habit of lugging around
human remains

Translation by Jennifer Scappettone

book

make love tenderly.

an open bridge across the river.

she kissed him for a while.

a field full of poppies and school graduation videotapes.

sky and sea the same blue.

the angel eloise plays a clip of audrey hepburn in *funny face*.

paloma is too sad.

during the berlin crisis.

she has brown antibiotics too, and a pocket vessel made of mineral coffee.

powered by the wind.

fifty-five rag dolls squeezed in one face starring marlon brando.

people sleeping in cars.

people burning cars.

libro

make love tenderly.

un ponte alzato aperto sul fiume.

lei bacia lui, per un po'.

un campo fitto di papaveri e di videocassette di cerimonie di laurea.

cielo e mare dello stesso blu.

l'angelo eloise fa un video di audrey hepburn in *funny face*.

paloma è troppo triste.

durante la crisi di berlino.

lei ha antibiotici marroni, anche, e un vascello tascabile fatto di caffè minerale.

spinto dal vento.

cinquantacinque bambole di pezza strizzate in una sola faccia, interpreta
marlon brando.

gente che dorme dentro le macchine.

gente che brucia macchine.

Translated by the author

***

1.

è molto facile contrarre la malattia e l'opposizione deve essere pronta fin dalle prime ore del mattino.

Non è molto semplice opporsi. Ma è il livello minimo (e anche massimo) di soluzione nota. Anche se, almeno fino a oggi, in realtà non è quasi mai stata una vera soluzione.

Una volta contratta, la malattia è in buona sostanza interna. Irreversibile e incurabile. Le persone siedono molte ore, specie parenti stretti, osservandosi e incolpandosi a vicenda senza parole del loro stato.

Ogni tanto il rumore di un'ambulanza un po' lontano un po' vicino ricorda dove si trovano, e che non è più un suono innocuo come quando, da borghesi, ridevano nel loro modo e mondo consueto.

Erano in pericolo.

7.

La sera andavano in via Veneto. Lì c'era un distributore di uranio aperto giorno e notte, e si diventava brillanti senza saperlo.

10.

è debole, non vuole nascere. Nascerebbe volentieri al contrario, verso il buio, sparato verso il buio. Nascerebbe all'indietro, al rovescio, a belle dosi, dormendo, a torcicollo, retrocedendo per non vedere, schivando i secchi di latta appesi, le funi per terra, le tagliole, le buatte scoperchiate, il marmo, i piani di pietra grigia, i cilindri che sono strutture di sedie e paglia, svuotando, à rebours, rewind, sempre cedendo verso il meno, verso il nero, verso una diminuzione non generata e non generale ma che è una *sua* diminuzione, un affievolirsi di unità, di uno solo, mancando, perdendo, via via, diminuendo come detto, sottratto, raccorciando, daccapo con meno materiali e personaggi, tosse e freddo, altra tosse più lontana, un freddo forte, sala vuota.

***

1.
It's very easy to catch the disease and resistance must be prompt from the first hours of the morning.

It's not easy to resist. But it is the minimal (or even maximal) degree of the acknowledged remedy. Even if, until now, there has never been in reality an actual remedy.

Once caught, the disease is essentially inside. Irreversible and incurable. The people sit for many hours, close relatives especially, observing and faulting one another without a word about their condition.

Every now and then the sound of an ambulance somewhat far away somewhat near reminds them of where they are, though it's no longer an innocuous noise as when, in plain clothes, they laughed in their own manner in the familiar world.

They were in danger.

7.
In the evening they went to Veneto street. There, there was a distributor of uranium open day and night, so they became brilliant without knowing it.

10.
Weak, he does not want to be born. He would gladly be born in reverse, towards the dark, shot towards the dark. He would rather be born backward, reversed, with an ample dosage, sleeping, stiff necked, recoiling to not see, dodging the hanging tin pails, ropes on the ground, traps, uncovered buckets, marble, grey rock floors, cylinders that are seating structures and straw, emptying, *à rebours, rewind*, always giving way towards less, towards black, towards a diminution neither generated nor general but a diminution that belongs to him, a waning of unity, of one only, lacking, letting go, away away, diminishing as stated, subtracted, shortening, once more with less stuff and personality, cough and chill, another cough further away, a pronounced chill, empty room.

11.

Sì, è come lei dice, mi sono rifiutato di ascoltare la musica, per la polvere. Sul disco, sì. Non ho neanche letto, nessuna lettera, per lo stesso motivo, appena, detto. Sono rimasto nel mio nascondiglio per tutto il tempo. Ho cercato di non imparare niente. Ho cercato di semplificare all'estremo le mie parole. In alcuni momenti la semplicità era perfino più forte della realtà. Pensavo di tradirla. Era pieno di macchie. Nessuno poteva verificare quello che dicevo. Quando fu trascritta dai cronisti la frase più celebre, relativa all'amore, molti non ne compresero l'oggetto. Per quanto semplificassi tutto, a rischio di mentire, non tutto per loro era chiaro. Quasi niente, anzi. Allora passando interamente sul fronte della menzogna pensai: ora sarà evidente, esplicito. Mentirò sempre, completamente, senza retorica. In modo piatto. Sarà decifrata ogni cosa. Intenderanno. Mi capiranno perché è il loro stesso linguaggio. Con tutta la sintassi azzerata, totalmente semplificata. Loro capiscono le bugie, le deformazioni. Leggeranno. Sarà limpido. Sbagliavo. Neanche così funzionò. Non funzionava.

11.

Yes, like you told me, I refused to listen to music, because of the dust. On the record, yes. I didn't even read, not even a letter, for the same reason, just as stated. Stayed in my hiding place the entire time. I tried not to learn anything. Tried to simplify to the utmost my words. At any moment simplicity was even stronger than reality. I thought I was betraying it. It was full of specks. No one could verify what I said. When it was transcribed by the reporters the most celebrated phrase, relative to love, many of them didn't understand the objective. Even if I simplified everything, at the risk of lying, not everything was clear to them. Nearly nothing, really. Now as I cross entirely into deception, I'm thinking: now it will be clear, explicit. I'll always lie, completely, without rhetoric. Plainly. Everything will be deciphered. They'll want it that way. They'll understand me because it's also their language. With all the syntax reduced to zero, totally simplified. They understand the lies, the distortions. They'll read. It will be clear. I was wrong. It didn't even work like that. It wasn't working.

Translated by Linh Dinh

MARIANGELA GUALTIERI

Mariangela Gualtieri was born in Cesena, Italy, in 1951 and trained as an architect. In 1983 she founded, together with Cesare Ronconi, the renowned Teatro Valdoca, where she works as playwright, actor, and director. Long committed to cultivating the oral dimension of poetry and its communal, collective roots, she routinely bridges the realms of poetry and theatre, as best evidenced by the collection *Fuoco centrale e altre poesie per il teatro* (Einaudi, 2003) and the theatrical text in verse, *Caino* (Einaudi, 2011).

Gualtieri's books include: *Antenata* (Crocetti, 1992); *Senza polvere senza peso* (Einaudi, 2006); *Paesaggio con fratello rotto* (Luca Sossella Editore, 2007); *Bestia di gioia* (Einaudi, 2010); *Sermone ai cuccioli della mia specie* (book and CD, Teatro Valdoca, 2012*); A Seneghe* with the photographer Guido Guidi (Perda Sonadora Imprentas, 2012); *Le giovani parole* (Einaudi, 2015); and *Beast of Joy: Selected Poems* (Chelsea Editions, New York, 2018). She is also a co-author of *Album e Tavole dei Giuramenti* (Quodlibet, 2019) and *Quando non morivo* (Einaudi, 2019).

TRANSLATORS

Anthony Molino is a practicing psychoanalyst, anthropologist, and literary translator. He has translated Mariangela Gualtieri, Valerio Magrelli, Lucio Mariani and Antonio Porta. Molino has also translated a number of Italian plays, including Eduardo De Filippo's *Natale in Casa Cupiello* and Manlio Santanelli's *Emergency Exit*.

Olivia E. Sears is the board president and founder of the Center for the Art of Translation. She co-founded the journal *Two Lines* in 1993. As a translator of Italian poetry, she focuses primarily on avant-garde poetry by women poets of the past hundred years, and the poetry of war.

Cristina Viti is a translator and poet working with Italian, English and French. Recent translations include Anna Gréki's *The Streets of Algiers* (Smokestack Books, 2020); Mariangela Gualtieri's *Beast of Joy* (Chelsea Editions, 2018); and Elsa Morante's *The World Saved by Kids* (Seagull Books, 2016), shortlisted for the John Florio Prize.

***

Sii dolce con me. Sii gentile.
E' breve il tempo che resta. Poi
saremo scie luminosissime.
E quanta nostalgia avremo
dell'umano. Come ora ne
abbiamo dell'infinità.
Ma non avremo le mani. Non potremo
fare carezze con le mani.
E nemmeno guance da sfiorare
leggere.

Una nostalgia d'imperfetto
ci gonfierà i fotoni lucenti.
Sii dolce con me.
Maneggiami con cura.
Abbi la cautela dei cristalli
con me e anche con te.
Quello che siamo
è prezioso più dell'opera blindata nei sotterranei
e affettivo e fragile. La vita ha bisogno
di un corpo per essere e tu sii dolce
con ogni corpo. Tocca leggermente
leggermente poggia il tuo piede
e abbi cura
di ogni meccanismo di volo
di ogni guizzo e volteggio
e maturazione e radice
e scorrere d'acqua e scatto
e becchettio e schiudersi o
svanire di foglie
fino al fenomeno
della fioritura,
fino al pezzo di carne sulla tavola
che è corpo mangiabile

***

Be gentle with me. Be kind.
Little is the time we have left. Then
we will be trails of pure light.
And so nostalgic
of the human. The way we now
are of infinity.
But we will not have hands. No longer
will we caress with our hands.
Nor cheeks to stroke,
softly.

Nostalgia of the imperfect
will swell our glowing photons.
Be gentle with me.
Handle me with care.
Me, and you too, with the caution
reserved to crystals.
What we are is more precious
than the contents of an underground vault,
and made of fragile feeling. Life needs
a body to be and you be gentle
with every body. Touch lightly
and lightly plant your foot
and take good care
of every mechanism of flight
of every swish and spin
every ripeness and root
and rush of water, all dashing
and pecking and unfolding
or fading of leaves
right up to the formula
of the flower
to the piece of meat on the table
body become edible

per il tuo mio ardore d'essere qui.
Ringraziamo. Ogni tanto.
Sia placido questo nostro esserci –
questo essere corpi scelti
per l'incastro dei compagni
d'amore.

for your, my, daring to be here.
Let us give thanks. Every now and then.
And may our being here be placid –
our being bodies chosen
partners in the fittings
of love.

Translation by Anthony Molino

***

Ormai è sazio di ferite e di cielo. Si chiama
uomo. Si chiama donna. È qui
nel celeste del pianeta
dice mamma. Dice cane
o aurora. La parola amore la ha inventata
intrappolato nel gelo, perso. Lontano. Solo.
L'ha scritta con ditate di rosso
in un silenzio caduto giù dalla neve.

***

It's had its fill of wounds and sky by now. Call it
man. Call it woman. Here it is
in the sky-blue of the planet
saying mama. Saying dog
or daybreak. The word love invented
while trapped in ice, while lost. Faraway. Alone.
Written with fingerfulls of red
in a silence that fell from the snow.

Translation by Cristina Viti

***

Sono stata una ragazza nel roseto
una ninfa. Quasi fantasma che stava
scomparendo
sono stata una ragazza di sedici anni
distesa. Ho attraversato il deserto
rapidamente, quasi volando,
una statua di pietra del Budda
dormiente, un Budda di cenere
sono stata. Una donna appesa.
Sono stata un uomo duro e forzuto.
Una eccentrica con un pesce in bocca
e poi il bambino dell'imperatore
del giardino orientale. Un albero
forse. Un topo. Un elefante
una lepre. Un intero pianeta.
Forse una stella un lago. Acqua sono
stata, questo lo so. Sono stata acqua
e vento. Una pioggia su qualcosa
che ero stata tempo addietro.
Forse anche il mare.
E dunque – di cosa dovrei avere paura
adesso.

***

I have been a girl in the rose garden
a nymph. A near-ghost
in a vanishing act
I've been a sixteen-year-old
lying down. I've crossed the desert
nimbly, nearly flying,
a stone statue of the sleeping
Buddha, I have been
a Buddha of ash. A woman dangling.
I have been a man, hard and brawny.
An eccentric with fish in mouth
and then the emperor's child
in the Oriental garden. Perhaps
a tree. A mouse. An elephant
a hare. An entire planet.
Perhaps a star, a lake. Water I've been
this I know. I've been water
and wind. Rain, on something
I'd been before.
Perhaps the sea as well.
And so – whatever should I fear
now.

Translation by Anthony Molino

***

La miglior cosa da fare stamattina
per sollevare il mondo e la mia specie
è di stare sul gradino al sole
con la gatta in braccio a far le fusa.
Sparpagliare le fusa
per i campi la valle
la collina, fino alle cime alle costellazioni
ai mondi più lontani. Far le fusa
con lei – la mia sovrana.
Imparare quel mantra che contiene
l'antica vibrazione musicale
forse la prima, quando dal buio immoto
per traboccante felicità
un gettito innescò la creazione.

***

The best thing to do this morning
to uplift the world and my species
is to sit on the step in the sun
with my cat in my lap, purring.
To scatter her purr
across the fields and valley
and hillside, unto mountaintops and constellations
to distant, faraway worlds. To purr
with her – my sovereign.
To learn the mantra that contains
the ancient musical vibration
the first, perhaps, when from the immote darkness
out of a swell of happiness
a spurt triggered the dawn of creation.

Translation by Anthony Molino

***

Per tutte le costole bastonate e rotte.
Per ogni animale sbalzato da suo nido
e infranto nel suo meccanismo d'amore.
Per tutte le seti che non furono saziate
fino alle labbra spaccate alla caduta
e all'abbaglio. Per i miei fratelli
nelle tane. E le mie sorelle
nelle reti e nelle tele e nelle
sprigionate fiamme e nelle capanne
e rinchiuse e martoriate. Per le bambine
mie strappate. E le perle nel fondale
marino. E per l'inverno che mi piace
e l'urlo della ragazza
quel suo tentare la fuga invano.

Per tutto questo conoscere e amare
eccomi. Per tutto penetrare e accogliere
eccomi. Per ondeggiare col tutto
e forse cadere eccomi
che ognuno dei semi inghiottiti
si farà in me fiore
fino al capogiro del frutto lo giuro.

Che qualunque dolore verrà
puntualmente cantato, e poi anche
quella leggerezza di certe
ore, di certe mani delicate, tutto sarà
guardato mirabilmente
ascoltata ogni onda di suono, penetrato
nelle sue venature ogni canto ogni pianto
lo giuro adesso che tutto è
impregnato di spazio siderale.
Anche in questa brutta città appare chiaro
sopra i rumorosissimi bar
lo spettro luminoso della gioia.
Questo lo giuro.

***

For all the ribs battered and broken.
For every animal hurled from its nest
its mechanism for love shattered.
For all the thirst left unquenched
until lips crack until collapse
until the glaring failure. For my brothers
in their dens. And my sisters
in traps and in their webs and in
the flames erupting and in their huts
and bound and abused. For the children
torn from me. And the pearls in the sea
bed. For the winter I adore
and for the girl's scream,
her vain attempt to flee.

For this, knowing and loving all this,
I am here. To fathom and embrace all this
I am here. To float along with everything
perhaps to fall I am here
so that every swallowed seed
will flower in me
until the fruit astonishes I swear it.

Let all suffering
be duly sung
so the lightness of certain
hours, of certain delicate hands, all
will be viewed with wonder
every wave of sound heard, every
song every sob will penetrate the veins
I swear now everything is
suffused with stars and space.
Even in this ugly city the glowing
spectre of joy shines bright
above the noisiest taverns.
This I swear.

Translation by Olivia E. Sears

ANDREA INGLESE

Andrea Inglese was born in Turin in 1967 and currently lives on the outskirts of Paris. He has a PhD in Comparative Literature and has held teaching positions in Contemporary Italian Literature at the University of Paris III. A poet, essayist, translator and novelist, he has also written theoretical as well as critical essays both in Italian and French.

He has published nine books of poetry and experimental prose. *Lettere alla Reinserzione Culturale del Disoccupato* has appeared in an Italian edition (Italic Pequod, 2013); as well as in French (NOUS, 2013); and English (*Letters to the Cultural Rehabilitation of the Unemployed*, Patrician Press, 2017). Among his latest publications are the collection of short proses *Ollivud* (Prufrock spa, 2018) and the prosimetrum *Mes Adieux à Andromède* (art&fiction, 2020).

His poetry has appeared in a variety of Italian contemporary poetry anthologies published in Italy and abroad. He has translated a number of French contemporary poets into Italian and edited an anthology by French poet Jean-Jacques Viton (*Il commento definitivo. Poesie 1984–2008*, Metauro, 2009). As a novelist he published *Parigi è un desiderio* (Bridge Prize 2017 for Fiction) and *La vita adulta* (Ponte alle Grazie, 2016 and 2020).

Inglese is a founding member of the distinguished literary blog, *Nazione Indiana* and is curating the project *Descrizione del mondo*, a collection of texts, sounds and images.

TRANSLATOR

Johanna Bishop is a translator of contemporary Italian poetry, fiction, non-fiction and art criticism. Her work has appeared extensively in the bilingual review *TheFLR*, as well as in other journals and anthologies, and recent books include *Tamam Shud*, a novel by visual artist Alex Cecchetti. She lives in Tuscany.

Il contorno, che prende tre lati solo, è a meandri con fondi oltremare, lacca e bigio, intorno al quale s'intrecciano festoncini di rose, che cadono in varie forme dalle volute ornamentali. All'interno, nello sgombro camerino, dove raccolgono le salamandre, gli scheletri spolpati di due: uno era intero intero, all'altro manca la coda. Quindici erano le costole laterali del busto in tutte e due. La mandibola tanto superiore quanto inferiore è armata di foltissime puntarelle o sia denti, coi quali le salamandre fermano la preda. Posate a terra, quattro gorgiere bianchissime, e un collaretto a ricamo. Nel cilindro graduato, semi di papavero e fieno greco. Dai tubi di sfiato, poco udibili, richiami di vittime docilissime, cerbiatti o bambini.

The border, which runs along three sides only, features a meander motif on an ultramarine, carmine and grey ground, intertwined with assorted festoons of roses that hang from the running ornament. Inside, in the small bare chamber, where the salamanders are kept, are two skeletons stripped of flesh: one all of a piece, the other lacking its tail. The ribs on either thorax number fifteen. Both the upper and lower jaws are armed with close-set protrusions or teeth with which the salamander seizes its prey. Lying on the ground are three snow-white ruffs, and an embroidered collarette. In the graduated cylinder, poppy seeds and fenugreek. From the vents, barely audible, come the calls of docile victims: children or young fawns.

Translation by Johanna Bishop

Cornice in racemi popolati da miriadi di animali: lucertole, rane, serpenti, passeri, vespe, coleotteri, chiocciole. Su ciascun lato l'asse della composizione è costituito da una candelabra sorgente da un grande cespo d'acanto, che genera da entrambi i lati una serie di ampie volute vegetali dove spighe di grano, capsule di papavero, rami di quercia, edera e vite nascono dallo stesso tralcio. All'interno del fregio, l'elegante esperimento di Worthington sulla caduta di un sasso tondo nell'acqua, con il formarsi dapprima di un cratere in superficie e quindi il sollevarsi d'una coppa laminare d'acqua tutt'intorno. Il bordo del cratere manifesta alternativamente dei solchi e delle sporgenze e i lobi o prominenze che si proiettano al di fuori tendono a rompersi in una serie di goccioline. La formazione del cratere indica che il liquido si solleva dal basso; la segmentazione del bordo produce zone di flusso facilitato, lungo le quali il liquido è portato a creare protuberanze che si allungano esageratamente. Dal cespo d'acanto del lato sud, sporge il busto di Andrew Kehoe, lo stragista della Bath School, a Bath Township, Michigan (45 morti & 58 feriti): la calotta completamente scoperchiata, ingigantita d'escrescenze, a cratere esploso.

Frame of scrollwork housing a myriad of animals: lizards, frogs, snakes, sparrows, wasps, beetles, snails. On both sides, the composition centres on a candelabrum rising from a large acanthus cluster; it branches left and right into a series of large volutes of foliage in which ears of wheat, poppy capsules, sprays of oak, ivy, and grape leaves spring from the same stem. Inside this frieze is Mr. Worthington's elegant experiment with the fall of a round pebble into water, causing the formation of a crater on the surface and the rise of a cup-like film of water all around. The edges of this crater are cut into alternate lobes and notches, or jets that shoot out and break up into droplets. The rise of the crater indicates that liquid is flowing up from below; the segmentation of the rim means that channels of easier flow are created, along which the liquid is driven into exaggerated protuberances. Rising out of the acanthus cluster on the south side is a bust of Andrew Kehoe, perpetrator of the Bath School Massacre in Bath Township, Michigan (45 dead & 58 wounded): crown of skull wide open, swollen by excrescences, in the style of an exploded crater.

Translation by Johanna Bishop

***

In questa poesia
la distruzione arriva molto lentamente
ma è una distruzione certa
che si concluderà d'un tratto

la distruzione procede in modo ponderato
con prudenza ma la sua
azione sarà efficace ed estrema

per questo motivo è stranissimo
che non se l'aspettino
con tutto il tempo che la distruzione prende
intorno a loro

se ne stanno seduti inattivi
devono essere almeno quattro a stento
riescono a parlare tanto sono quieti
attorno al tavolo con i loro bicchieri
gli album fotografici da sfogliare

non che siano tristi o svuotati
si godono il pomeriggio con totale
fedeltà hanno ancora molte lettere
da scrivere e viaggi da organizzare

ma neppure per un attimo li sfiora
una minima apprensione o l'idea
che sebbene lenta la distruzione scende
a raggio vastissimo inesorabile

io vorrei dirglielo in qualche modo
all'interno della poesia lasciar emergere
un segnale inequivocabile di pericolo
ma tutti e quattro sono così assorti

***

In this poem
destruction arrives very slowly
but it is certain destruction
that will come to a head all at once

destruction proceeds with all due prudence
circumspectly but its action
will be thorough and extreme

that's why it is so strange
that none of them expect it
considering how long the destruction is taking
all around them

they're just sitting there idle
four of them at least they're hardly able
to keep up a conversation so very tranquil
around the table sitting with their drinks
with photo albums to page through

not that they're feeling sad or drained
they're savouring the afternoon with total
devotion there are still so many letters
to be written and trips to be organised

but not even for a second are they grazed
by the slightest apprehension or the thought
that however slow destruction is descending
in a measureless inexorable radius

I would like to tell them somehow
in this poem let some hint slip out
an unmistakable signal of danger
but all four are so deeply engrossed

si conoscono bene sono di famiglia
hanno legami stretti non sentono l'urgenza
di guardarsi attorno con sospetto
o di prendere la parola in affanno

la distruzione per come viene
con il suo moto languido
certo non li risparmia
il punto d'impatto anzi

se guardiamo dall'alto
è ubicato al centro della loro
sala da pranzo

they know each other well they're family
they're all very close they feel no urgent need
to look around them with any suspicion
or to speak up in frantic concern

given how destruction comes
the way it moves so languidly
of course they won't be spared
in point of fact ground zero

if we look down from above
is located at the very centre of their
dining room

Translation by Johanna Bishop

***

In questa poesia
avvenimenti accadono alle persone
e le persone raggiungono una zona di sicurezza
è un grosso ininterrotto lavoro
molto più del lavoro
sono più delle 40 o 50 ore settimanali
non si tratta di ricchezza
è un lavoro dietro al lavoro
la zona di sicurezza implica una minuziosa migrazione
si calcola in spanne giornaliere
si perdono i capelli s'ingrossano le coronarie
è un felicità dietro la felicità
sono emozioni più lente
le percepisci vagamente
come un centimetro quadrato di costa
che si forma nel corso di un secolo
ci stanno lavorando dal tempo dei bisnonni
e prima ancora
la zona dovrebbe essere segnalata
non può per definizione essere selvaggia
apri gli occhi e scoverai i vialetti puliti il quadro
delle luci le tubature rifatte
il biglietto di benvenuto dei vicini
i passanti sono dispensati dal rivolgerti la parola
non sarai tu a raccogliere il porcospino schiacciato
o le prugne sull'uscio di casa
e comunque
la zona di sicurezza
alla fine le persone lo sospettano
è una banchisa mobile e crepata
l'importante è che sia larga quanto basta
e la tua vita breve quanto basta

***

In this poem
events happen to people
and people reach a safety zone
it's a massive unremitting job
much more than any job
more than those 40 or 50 hours a week
it's not about prosperity
it's a job behind the job
the safety zone involves a meticulous migration
calculated in daily increments
you lose your hair your arteries start to harden
it's a happiness behind happiness
emotions of a slower kind
you feel them only vaguely
a square inch of coastline growing
over the course of a century
they've been working on it since your great-grandfather's day
and even before that
the zone must be marked out somehow
by definition it can't be wild
open your eyes and you'll find the footpaths swept the breaker
box the plumbing all redone
the note of welcome from the neighbours
passers-by are exempted from speaking to you
you won't be the one to gather up the flattened hedgehog
or the plums outside the door
and anyway
the safety zone
as everyone comes to suspect
is a moving, fissured ice floe
all that matters is that it be wide enough
and your life short enough

Translation by Johanna Bishop

***

In questa poesia
per salire sulla magnolia servono bambini
che poi sposteremo nella serra
a cercare ragni e mosconi morti nelle vasche
di terra brulla
cammineranno sullo stretto muro di recinzione carponi
fin nella villa fatiscente
scavando una via tra ortiche cardi convolvoli giganti
nell'atrio tutte le finestre infrante
i materassi al primo piano le pagine incollate
gli aloni neri di fiamma sulle pareti
qualcuno potrà trovare
una teiera alla sassone un manuale di ciclismo
un cilindro svasato di ottone forse
strumento di precisione
arma da parata
o reliquia borghese
di un rituale erotico

qualcosa si lascerà sottotitolato invisibile
ultrasonico: uno svolazzare pallido
di antichi strazi carezze vaghe
lungo le piastrelle del bagno
la grande riflessione sul sonno
i pianori di tutte le dimenticanze
il tempio sempre oscillante della sparizione

***

In this poem
to climb the magnolia we need children
who will later be moved to the greenhouse
to look for dead spiders and flies in the tubs
of barren earth
they will move along the narrow outer wall on hands and knees
all the way to the crumbling villa
carving out a path through nettles thistles giant bindweed
in the entrance all the windows shattered
the mattresses upstairs the pages glued together
the black haloes of flame across the panelling
somebody may find
a Dresden-style teapot a cycling manual
a flared brass cylinder that could be a
precision instrument
parade weapon
or bourgeois relic
of an erotic rite

something will be left as an invisible
ultrasonic subtitle: a pale fluttering
of ancient torments vague caresses
down the bathroom tiles
the great reflection on slumber
the tablelands of all forgetfulness
the ever swaying temple of disappearances.

Translation by Johanna Bishop

ROSARIA LO RUSSO

Rosaria Lo Russo is a poet, performer, translator and essayist born in Florence in 1964, where she still lives. Her poetry collections include *L'estro* (Cesati, 1987); *Vrusciamundo* (I quaderni del Battello Ebbro, 1994); *Comedia* (Bompiani, 1998); *Penelope* (d'if, 2003); *Lo dittatore amore. Melologhi* (Effigie, 2004); *Io e Anne. Confessional poems* (d'if, 2010); *Crolli* (Le Lettere, 2012); *Poema (1990/2000)* (Zona, 2013); *Nel nosocomio* (Effigie, 2016); *Controlli*, published with Daniele Vergni in a book and DVD format (Millegru, 2016, Elio Pagliarani Prize in 2017); *Anatema* (Effigie, 2021); and *Rina* (Battello Stampatore, 2021).

As a translator, Lo Russo has published four books of Anne Sexton's poetry: *Love Poems* (Poesie d'amore, Le Lettere, 1996, second revised edition, 2019); *L'estrosa abbondanza* (anthology with Edoardo Zuccato and Antonello Satta Centanin, 1997); *Poesie su Dio* (Le Lettere, 2003); and *The Book of Folly* (*Il libro della follia*, La nave di Teseo, 2021).

As an essayist Lo Russo has written *Figlia di solo padre* (Seri Editore, 2020) and *La protagonista di Pirandello* (Metauro, 2021). Since 2000 she has voiced Dante's *Commedia* with her show *Voci in Comedia. Lectura Dantis.* She has also voiced many other poets including Bigongiari, Luzi, Pagliarani, Brodskij, Caproni, Zanzotto, Szymborska, Vicinelli, Balestrini, Calogero, and Rosselli (see CD and DVD *La furia dei venti contrari. Variazioni Amelia Rosselli*, edited by A. Cortellessa, Le Lettere, 2007).

TRANSLATORS

Serena Todesco is a literary translator and scholar of Italian literature, specialising in southern Italian women writers (Elena Ferrante, Anna Maria Ortese, Michela Murgia and Maria Rosa Cutrufelli). She has collaborated with several poetry festivals in Italy, Ireland and Croatia.

William Wall is an Irish novelist, poet and short-story writer. In 1997, Wall won the Patrick Kavanagh Poetry Award. He published his first collection of poetry in that year. He is the author of four novels, two collections of poetry and one of short stories.

***

Le cose, bistrattate dai molti sgomberi, mi serbano rancore.
Si schiudono crepe lendini prudenti
suggerendo future aliene infestazioni.
Calano i festoni di un vecchio compleanno
come occhiaie improvvisate da un dolore
immenso e subitaneo come una complanare.
Vorrei paragonare queste serbate crepe
a quelle di genti vicine che da poco fa furono in guerra
là per dove le cose che fecero festa sgualciscono,
ma anche a una subìta lacrima di perdenti.
Ma a tutto ci si attacca e dappertutto depongo
furtivamente armi da invasata:
e tu non mi guardare mentre in vitro
suppotenti confluiamo in guerre molto civili.

***

Things, disowned and badly treated, bear me a grudge.
Itching nits hatch from cracks,
suggesting future alien infestations.
The drooping streamers of some old birthday
like eye-bags improvised of pain
immense, abrupt like a coplanar.
I'd liken these gathering rifts
to those of our neighbours recently at war,
there where the party-things are crumbling,
but also to a loser's tolerated tear.
But one becomes attached to things and everywhere
I lay down arms furtively like one possessed
and you, don't you look at me, while, in vitro,
superpresumptuous, we flow together into very civil wars.

Translation by Serena Todesco and William Wall

***

Così ci rubano – rimetta – l'antica lingua
disseminando babilonie come scrollassero di dosso
torri babelliche che confuse sparigliano
idiomi suppellettili in snervanti soprammobili da spolvero.
Così spossando un arduo deserto fecondo
scendono a bomba a bomba nell'arena assolta,
disanimati gladiatori ebbri d'attrezzi.
Arrugginisce la tenaglia del tenace delta,
che si biforca ruggendo ai nostri barbari.
Così gli invasi emulano all'armi
chi, inimicandosi, scompiglia supplici incartamenti
d'orecchie con spocchie fluorescenti al fosforo.
E non sappiamo chi intimamente ci scommetta.

***

Thus they steal – little rhyme – our ancient tongue
disseminating babylons as if shaking
off babellicose towers, mindlessly reducing
idioms to weary ornaments of dust.
Exhausting the brutal fertile desert
descending bomb by bomb on the purged arena,
disheartened gladiators high on gear.
The rusting pincer of the stubborn delta,
bifurcate, bays at our barbarians.
Thus the invaded emulate with arms,
the alien who disturbs the begging dog-eared papers
with fluorescing phosphorous conceits.
And no one knows who secretly has money on it.

Translation by Serena Todesco and William Wall

***

Otturare le crepe, cremare i cadaveri, sbuffa
imponendo: polvere alla polvere, e le ceneri siano
disperse ridisegnando reticoli di lumi a questi
barbuti neroni! Mammaliturchi annuncia l'annunciatrice
insomma, scaltra ammiccando uno sconto di civiltà
per chi imbiancasse poveri da spolvero, per chi l'aria
da funerale e bocche disfatte da manomorte
manomettesse pure, o ponzipilati d'un altro canale.
Evacuare i canili degli sfidanti sfedeli,
rastrellare adozioni avide distanza d'infanti,
ripristinare i canili per sfacciare incappucciati,
tornare alla lingua di casa una volta stravinto un vuoto.

***

Closing the cracks, burning the corpses, snorting
with haste: dust to dust, and the ashes to be
scattered, contriving fences of enlightenment for these
black-bearded Neroes! Mamma mia, the Turks! announces the announcer,
in short, nods and winks for the Clash of Civilisations
for those whitewashing the dusty poor, for whom
there is the funeral lament and the mouths closed by dead hands
or even by fiddling the system, oh pontiuspilates from some other channel.
And to empty the kennels of these defiant heretics
long-distance adoptions pillage infants,
other kennels are prettified for the faceless hooded ones,
while the mother-tongue calls home the conqueror from the void.

Translation by Serena Todesco and William Wall

A Luigi Nacci, sodale

Dicevo insomma riga dritto il fronte compatto dei dementi
niente di nuovo alletta il fronte occidentale:
le fronti coperte di pelle in polvere corrugano,
diserbando, staccando arbusti, e vane colluttazioni,
a cedimenti di guance smunte, gli ultravioletti
di guerra corruschi annunciano signorine mezzobusto,
con povere alla polvere ceneri nonviolente di dispersi,
pinchi pallini bifidi tra infidi batteri, tu spàrati un
paradiso artificiale e restaci se hai il coraggio
di circondarti di veline scure, irsute e insistenti scassa-
arpe metriche e petecchie, dardi codardi, avanzi pimpanti
di guantanamera, bandiera rossa, faccetta nera.

To Luigi Nacci, brother

To recapitulate: it forms up well The Front Of the Demented;
nothing new, once again, attracts The Western Front;
dust corrugates the leather-covered foreheads,
defoliating, wrecking plants, fruitless brawls,
collapsing of gaunt cheeks, the ultraviolet
flashes of war announced by Miss Talking Head,
with the dust-to-destitute nonviolent ashes of the dispersed,
joebloggs wounded among renegade germs, fix yourself
your artificial paradise and stay there if you're brave enough
surrounding yourself with obscure showgirls, pushy toupéed culture-
mongers, petty measurers, wimpish shafters, pimpish leftovers
of Guantanamera, The Red Flag, or Faccetta Nera*.

Translation by Serena Todesco and William Wall

---

* '*Faccetta Nera*' ('Little Black Face') is an Italian fascist marching song. 'Little black face, little Abyssinian, we will bring you to Rome and liberate you, You will be kissed by our sun, you will wear a black shirt specially for you...'

***

Irreparabilmente puerili grandi occhi
circondano invasori un vuoto statico,
antefatto d'una discesa agli inferi
senza sospensioni della pena.
Subodora nel vuoto d'aria del risveglio
una perdita crema di saliva sul cuscino.
Le cose còlte sul fatto impertinente, da lato,
imperturbabili espongono penombre e pieghe
incrinate come rughe d'espressione.
Le crepe simmetricamente segnalano
rischi di selvatiche estinzioni o cadùcei
fulminanti peritoniti d'intonaco. Rimbomba
un sordido risveglio, riassopendosi.
Riassorbono le cose indispettite
due occhi glabri di basso sospetto,
alla risibile missionaria ripudiata
dall'irresistibile ascesa di una borghesia
come dalla borghesia in rapida discesa.

***

Irreparably boyish big eyes
invade a static emptiness,
indicate a descent into the underworld
without respite of punishment.
Undersmells in the aerial emptiness of waking
a wasted froth of saliva on the pillow.
Impertinent things taken unawares,
Imperturbable, expose pleats and eclipses,
cracked like frowns.
The crevices symmetrically signal
risks of species extinctions or caducei,
a fulminating peritonitis of plaster, a roaring
sordid arousing, re-drowsing.
The gloomy things reabsorbing
two vexed suspicious glances
at the risible repudiated missionary lady
from the irresistibly ascending bourgeoisie
as if from the bourgeoisie in decline and fall.

Translation by Serena Todesco and William Wall

VALERIO MAGRELLI

Valerio Magrelli was born in Rome in 1957. A Professor of French literature at the University of Pisa and then Cassino, he is also a frequent contributor to the cultural pages of Italian daily paper *La Repubblica*. He is the author of six poetry collections: *Ora serrata retinae* (Feltrinelli, 1980); *Nature e venature* (Mondadori, 1987); *Esercizi di tiptologia* (Mondadori, 1992); *Didascalie per la lettura di un giornale* (Einaudi, 1999); *Disturbi del sistema binario* (Einaudi, 2006); and *Il sangue amaro* (Einaudi, 2014). All these books were collected in *Le cavie* (Einaudi, 2018). His poems have been translated into several languages.

Magrelli's work has been published in English in several collections, including *Nearsights: Selected Poems* (translated by A. Molino, Graywolf Press, 1991); *The Contagion of Matter* (translated by A. Molino, Holmes & Meyer, 2000); *Instructions on How to Read a Newspaper, and Other Poems* (translated by Anthony Molino, Riccardo Duranti and Annamaria Crowe Serrano, Chelsea Editions, New York, 2008); *The Embrace* (translated by Jamie McKendrick, Faber & Faber, 2009, winner of the Oxford-Weidenfeld Prize and the John Florio Prize); *Vanishing Points* (bilingual edition of *The Embrace*, published by Farrar, Straus and Giroux, 2010); *The Secret Ambition* (translated by Douglas Reid Skinner and Marco Fazzini, African Sun Press, Cape Town, 2015); and *The Condominium of the Flesh* (translated by Clarissa Botsford, Parlor Press, Anderson, South Carolina, 2016).

TRANSLATORS

Jamie McKendrick is a poet and translator. He is the editor of *The Faber Book of 20th-century Italian Poems* (Faber, 2004). He translated Magrelli's *The Embrace* (Faber & Faber, 2009, winner of the Oxford-Weidenfeld Prize and the John Florio Prize). He has also translated Antonella Anedda's poems in *Tempo*.

Anthony Molino is a practicing psychoanalyst, anthropologist, and literary translator. He has translated Mariangela Gualtieri, Valerio Magrelli, Lucio Mariani and Antonio Porta. Molino has also translated a number of Italian plays, including Eduardo De Filippo's *Natale in Casa Cupiello* and Manlio Santanelli's *Emergency Exit*.

***

Scivola la penna
verso l'inguine della pagina,
ed in silenzio si raccoglie la scrittura.
Questo foglio ha i confini geometrici
di uno stato africano,
in cui disegno
i filari paralleli delle dune.
ormai sto disegnando
mentre racconto ciò
che raccontando si profila.
È come se una nube
arrivasse ad avere
forma di nube.

***

The pen slides
down the groin of the page,
while writing collects itself in silence.
This page has the geometry
of an African country,
where I map
out rows of parallel dunes.
Drawing
as I talk
what my tale prefigures.
As if a cloud
were to assume
the form of a cloud.

Translation by Anthony Molino

***

Di sera quando è poca la luce
nascosto dentro il letto
colgo i profili dei ragionamenti
che scorrono sul silenzio delle membra.
E' qui che devo tessere
l'arazzo del pensiero
e disponendo i fili di me stesso
disegnare con me la mia figura.
Questo non è un lavoro
ma una lavorazione.
Della carta prima, poi del corpo.
Suscitare la forma del pensiero,
sagomarla secondo una misura.

Penso ad un sarto
che sia la sua stessa stoffa.

***

Evenings, when the light dims
and I lie hidden in bed,
I gather outlines of ideas
that flow over the silence of my limbs.
It's here I must weave
thought's tapestry,
arrange my own strands
use myself to draw my own figure.
This isn't work
but workmanship.
Of the page, then of the body.
To evoke thought's form,
measure and fit it.

I think of a tailor
who is his own fabric.

Translation by Anthony Molino

***

Che la materia provochi il contagio
se toccata nelle sue fibre ultime
recisa come il vitello dalla madre
come il maiale dal proprio cuore
stridendo nel vedere le sue membra strappate;

Che tale schianto generi
la stessa energia che divampa
quando la società si lacera, sacro velo del tempio
e la testa del re cade spiccata dal corpo dello stato
affinché il taumaturgo diventi la ferita;

Che l'abbraccio del focolare sia radiazione
rogo della natura che si disgrega
inerme davanti al sorriso degli astanti
per offrire un lievissimo aumento
della temperatura ambientale;

Che la forma di ogni produzione
implichi effrazione, scissione, un addio
e la storia sia l'atto del combùrere
e la Terra una tenera catasta di legname
messa a asciugare al sole,

è incredibile, no?

***

That matter engenders contagion
if interfered with in its deepest fibres
cut out from its mother like a veal calf
like the pig from its own heart
screaming at the sight of its torn entrails;

That this destruction generates
the same energy that blazes out
when society turns on itself, the temple's veil torn
and the king's head axed from the body of the state
until the faith healer becomes the wound;

That the hearth's embrace is radiation
nature's pyre which unravels
helplessly before the smiling company
so as to effect the slightest increase
of the surrounding temperature;

That the form of every production implies
breaking and entry, fission, a final leavetaking
and that history is the act of combustion
and the Earth a tender stockpile of firewood
left out to dry in the sun,

is hard to credit is it not?

Translation by Jamie McKendrick

L'abbraccio

Tu dormi accanto a me così io mi inchino
e accostato al tuo viso prendo sonno
come fa lo stoppino
da uno stoppino che gli passa il fuoco.
E i due lumini stanno
mentre la fiamma passa e il sonno fila.
Ma mentre fila vibra
la caldaia nelle cantine.
Laggiù si brucia una natura fossile,
là in fondo arde la Preistoria, morte
torbe sommerse, fermentate,
avvampano nel mio termosifone.
In una buia aureola di petrolio
la cameretta è un nido riscaldato
da depositi organici, da roghi, da liquami.

E noi, stoppini, siamo le due lingue
di quell'unica torcia paleozoica.

The Embrace

As you lie beside me I edge closer
taking sleep from your lips
as one wick draws flame from another.
And two night-lights are lit
as the flame passes
between us. But as it passes
the boiler in the basement shudders:
down there a fossil nature burns,
down in the depths prehistory's
sunken fermented peats blaze up
and slither through my radiator.
Wreathed in a dark halo of oil,
the bedroom is a close nest
heated by organic deposits,
by log pyres, leafmash, seething resins…

And we are the wicks, the two tongues
flickering on that single Palaeozoic torch.

Translation by Jamie McKendrick

L'imballatore

Cos'è la traduzione? Su un vassoio
la testa pallida e fiammante d'un poeta
— V. Nabokov

L'imballatore chino
che mi svuota la stanza
fa il mio stesso lavoro.
Anch'io faccio cambiare casa
alle parole, alle parole
che non sono mie,
e metto mano a ciò
che non conosco senza capire
cosa sto spostando.
Sto spostando me stesso
traducendo il passato in un presente
che viaggia sigillato
racchiuso dentro pagine
o dentro casse con la scritta
'Fragile' di cui ignoro l'interno.
È questo il futuro, la spola, il traslato,
il tempo manovale e citeriore,
trasferimento e tropo,
la ditta di trasloco.

Removals Man

What is translation? The pale, flaming
head of the poet on a platter.
— V. Nabokov

The weighed-down removals man
who empties my room
does the same work as me.
I too arrange house removals
for words, for words
which aren't mine,
and lay hands on
what's beyond me
without quite figuring out
what it is I'm moving.
I am moving myself,
translating the past into a present
which travels sealed
and folded in pages
or in boxes labelled FRAGILE
about whose contents I can only guess.
And this is the future, the shuttle
moving back and forth, the metaphor,
labourer time, time with its hither zone,
its middle west or east,
almost within reach,
transferral and trope,
the removals firm.

Translated by Jamie McKendrick

GUIDO MAZZONI

Guido Mazzoni is a poet, scholar and literary critic born in Florence in 1967. He teaches at the University of Siena and lives in Rome. He has written three poetry collections: *La scomparsa del respiro dopo la caduta* (in *Terzo quaderno italiano*, ed. by Franco Buffoni, Guerini, 1992); *I mondi* (Donzelli, 2010); and *La pura superficie* (Donzelli, 2017); which won The Pagliarani Prize and the Napoli Prize in 2018. Mazzoni's poetry transcends the barrier of verse and prose, seeking an impossible point of contact between the fate of the individual and the large-scale collective events.

Mazzoni is the author of three books of literary theory: *Forma e solitudine* (Marcos y Marcos, 2002); *Sulla poesia moderna* (Il Mulino, 2005); and *Teoria del romanzo* (Il Mulino, 2011); later translated into English as *Theory of the Novel* (Harvard University Press, 2017). He has also published a book on contemporary politics and society, *I destini generali* (Laterza, 2015).

TRANSLATORS

Jacob Still Deutsch Blakesley is an American translator of fiction and poetry who teaches at the University of Leeds, where he co-directs the Leeds Centre for Dante Studies. He won a 2018 NEA Literature Translation Fellowship for a project on translating the modern experimental Italian poet Edoardo Sanguineti.

Dylan J. Montanari studied at the University of Chicago and Stanford University. He is the translator of *The Life of Plants: A Metaphysics of Mixture* by Emanuele Coccia (Polity Press, 2018), and he has published reviews in the *Los Angeles Review of Books*. He currently works at the University of Chicago Press.

Essere con gli altri

L'opacità degli altri mentre vi vengono incontro
per porre limiti, per definirvi, letteralmente. Siamo a disagio con loro,
usiamo le frasi per nascondere o mediare, le parole,
tutte le parole, sono un appello o un'aggressione, anche queste.

Incontra la madre di un'amica di sua figlia, si conoscono poco,
passano un pomeriggio al parco a sorvegliare le bambine, ogni cosa
sopra la panchina genera disagio. Si guarda le dita dei piedi,
i capelli sfibrati, c'è un confronto fra loro,
usa le sillabe come una protesi
mentre immagina sua figlia con ambivalenza,
il dottorato interrotto, i propri limiti.
È solo quando l'altra donna si indebolisce, quando racconta
di un fibroma o di una vita provinciale
che qualcosa può unirle. Poi le figlie tornano,
distruggono questo momento, vogliono il gelato.

Più tardi, mentre guida e guarda i cartelloni, la memoria
del pomeriggio si scompone
in una specie di liquido mentale: non ricorda.
Ieri un uomo giaceva a terra investito da un taxi,
era cosciente, aspettava l'ambulanza, aveva fra le mani
una busta con la scritta «Birkenstock». L'emorragia
lo allontanava da noi che restavamo eretti
e guardavamo il corpo sopra il marciapiede,
il sangue che esce dalla pelle, un'esistenza aliena.
Spesso nei vostri volti io vedo una distanza pura,
un'esteriorità assoluta.
                    Mette a letto la figlia,
ripensa al fibroma, al fastidio con cui ha guardato
le bambine mentre ritornavano, la vita degli altri
è bianca e spettrale, non ricorda.

Being-with-others

The opacity of others as they come toward you
to set limits, to define you, literally. We're ill-at-ease with them,
we use sentences to conceal or mediate, words,
all words, are either plea or aggression – even these.

She meets her daughter's friend's mother, they barely know each other,
they spend an afternoon at the park watching over the girls, everything
on that park bench generates unease. She looks at her toes,
her worn hair, there's a confrontation between them,
she uses syllables as a prosthesis
while she imagines her daughter ambivalently,
the dissertation put on hold, her own limits.
It's only when the other woman grows weak, when she speaks
of a fibroma or of provincial life
that something brings them together. Then the daughters return,
destroying the moment, asking for ice cream.

Later, while she drives, gazing at the billboards, the memory
of the afternoon decomposes
into a sort of mental liquid: she can't remember.
Yesterday a man was on the ground, hit by a taxi,
he was awake, waiting for the ambulance, holding
an envelope with 'Birkenstock' written on it. The hemorrhage
was distancing him from us, standing erect
and looking at the body on the sidewalk,
the blood leaving the skin, an alien existence.
Often, in your faces, I see pure distance,
absolute exteriority.
                    She puts her daughter to sleep,
thinks again about the fibroma, about the annoyance in her eyes
at the girls when they came back, the life of others
is white and ghostly, she can't remember.

Translation by Dylan Joseph Montanari

Étoile

Questa persona non significa nulla per te. La penetri per inerzia,
per la logica della serata, quasi tutto ti sfugge,
l'angoscia che provi al risveglio vuol dire che sei solo.
Nel dormiveglia ricordi le unghie imperfette,
i liquidi sulle coperte, le crepe che si aprono
fra le parole che hai detto, fra le parole
che non hai detto, i dettagli
di questa persona, la sua irrealtà, la sua orrenda
patina dialettale. È il giorno dopo,

i passeggeri, sulla linea sei, portano fuori i propri volti,
le nuvole sfiorano i vagoni, dal vetro si coglie
la natura di scatola, di riparo, delle case umane.
Da qualche tempo gli eventi scivolano sopra di me,
non mi toccano. Su questo lato
sono con voi, un altro scorre dentro,
è invisibile e mi sovrasta.
Ho proseguito oltre l'ultima fermata,
Étoile, senza una ragione,
guardavo gli altri, volevo distruggere o capire.

Étoile

This person means nothing to you. You penetrate her out of inertia,
according to the evening's logic, almost everything passes you by,
the anguish you feel upon waking means you are alone.
In your drowsy state you remember the imperfect nails,
the liquids on the sheets, the crevices that open up
between the words you said, between the words
you didn't say, the details
of this person, her unreality, the horrible
patina of her accent. It's the day after,

the passengers, on the 6 line, take their faces out,
clouds graze the train cars, from the window you see
the box-like, sheltering nature of human houses.
It's been some time now that events slide over me,
they don't touch me. On this side,
I am with you, another flows within,
it's invisible and overwhelming me.
I went past the last stop,
Étoile, for no reason,
I was watching the others, I wanted to destroy or understand.

Translation by Dylan Joseph Montanari

Sedici soldati siriani

Lo psicoanalista gli consiglia di non guardare immagini al risveglio, di svegliarsi lentamente per «recuperare il significato della propria presenza», ma l'Isis, nel sonno, ha decapitato sedici soldati siriani e li ha messi su Liveleak, e lui ora vuole vederli.

Un gruppo di miliziani trascina i prigionieri per il collo della tuta. La definizione è altissima, le luci sono scelte bene, gli uomini dell'Isis vogliono sembrare statue, i siriani vogliono sembrare umili; rasati e truccati guardano fissi nella camera mentre il regista inquadra la scena dal basso verso l'alto usando il rallentato per creare qualcosa che stia fra il monumento e il film d'azione. I prigionieri camminano piegati in due come ovipari, come paperi senza proporzione; un tizio vestito di nero spiega in inglese perché verranno uccisi. Guardano verso di noi da una regione interna remota con una specie di intensità teatrale, come se questa non fosse la loro vita. Poi il tizio smette di parlare, i miliziani tirano fuori i coltelli, i siriani vengono spinti a terra. Sono docili; vengono sgozzati con lo stesso movimento con cui si affetta la carne nel piatto, muovendo la lama avanti e indietro, infantilmente; e anche se il sangue esce a spruzzo l'inquadratura resta perfetta, l'ultimo prigioniero dissanguato fa in tempo a guardarci di nuovo prima di perdere coscienza. Poi c'è uno stacco, c'è un effetto di montaggio dopo il quale le teste dei siriani ricompaiono scisse dal corpo, poggiate sulle schiene, e parte la sigla di chiusura. È un video orribile. È un video molto bello. Significa molte cose – per esempio che l'avete visto, che avete desiderato vederlo, che uccidere un nemico è un gesto umano e vi appartiene, e chi sa compierlo è forte, più forte di chi lo guarda mentre fa colazione in una società esteriormente pacifica, occultamente crudele. Mette via il computer, finisce di mangiare.

La sera esce con un gruppo di persone che per abitudine chiama amici. Hanno più di quarant'anni, si conoscono superficialmente, come succede fra gli adulti; in mezzo a loro c'è un ventenne maschio ignoto. Gli ultraquarantenni sono qualcosa, hanno qualcosa e lo difendono (una coppia, un figlio, dei luoghi comuni, la possibilità stessa di parlarne seriamente); il maschio giovane non è niente e dunque è libero, parla senza sfumature, come se cercasse di incidere o tagliare, come se nulla avesse peso. Lui lo guarda fisso, lo odia intimamente. Vorrebbe essere così. Lo è stato venticinque anni fa; poi è diventato più umano,

Sixteen Syrian soldiers

His analyst advises him not to look at images when he wakes up, to get up slowly, to 'recover the meaning of his own presence', yet while he sleeps ISIS decapitated sixteen Syrian soldiers and put them on Liveleak, and he wants to see them now.

A group of militiamen drag along the prisoners by the collar of their uniforms. The images are ultra HD, the lights have been efficiently chosen, the ISIS combatants try to appear to be statues, the Syrians try to seem humble; shaved and made up, they stare at the camera while the director frames the scene from the bottom up, using slow-motion to create something half-way between a documentary and an action movie. The prisoners walk hunched over like oviparous creatures, like ducks without proportion; a guy dressed in black explains in English why they will be killed. They look towards us from a remote inner region, with a kind of theatrical intensity, as if this wasn't their life. Then the guy stops talking, the militiamen bring out their knives, the Syrians are pushed to the ground. They're docile: their throats are cut with the same movement with which one slices meat on a plate, moving the blade forwards and backwards, childishly; and even if the blood does flow in spurts, the framing is perfect, the last prisoner bleeding to death manages to look at us again before losing consciousness. Then there is a gap, there's an effect of montage after which the heads of the Syrians reappear separated from their bodies, placed on their backs, and the theme song starts up. It's a horrible video. It's a very beautiful video. It means many things – for example, that you've seen it, that you wanted to see it, that killing an enemy is a human act and belongs to you, and that whoever can do it is strong, stronger than whoever watches it while eating breakfast in a society outwardly peaceful, inwardly cruel. He puts away his computer, finishes eating.

That evening he goes out with a group of people whom he calls, from habit, his friends. They're all in their forties, they know each other superficially, as happens with adults; among them is a twenty-year-old, an unknown guy. The over-forty-year-olds are something, have something and they protect it (a couple, a son, stereotypes, the very possibility of speaking about them seriously); the younger man is nothing and thus is free, while speaking without subtleties, as though he meant to cut or slice, as though nothing had any weight. He stares at the younger

meno lucido, più indulgente, e oggi lascia che il maschio giovane si prenda il centro della scena parlando con disprezzo di un lavoro precario che lo mette vicino alle persone medie, quelle che pensano di essere qualcosa, assurdamente.

Poi la cena finisce e si apre quel momento in cui, dopo i saluti, guardando le case, le proprie scarpe o i cassonetti del vetro, si capisce che gli altri non ci riguardano o non ci interessano. Accompagna a casa una donna con cui ha un rapporto senza impegno. Lei si sta attaccando più di quanto hanno stabilito, lui si protegge fingendo di non capire. Scopano. Comincia un dialogo dove le parole significano altro, un discorso obliquo e pieno di rancore che ogni coppia conosce e che non vi descrivo; va avanti per ore mentre la mente si riempie di residui: le tute dei prigionieri, il maschio giovane, il gesto di tagliare, una pletora di dettagli, alla periferia della coscienza, che non sapeva di avere trattenuto. Pensa a un'auto, a un episodio della propria adolescenza, a una parola che non c'entra niente come «esantematico» o «organolettico»; pensa alle piante e agli animali piccoli, agli insetti per esempio, a come ogni loro corpo esista in uno sciame e scompaia senza enfasi, senza credere di essere qualcosa. È orribile. È orribile ma non importa.

man, he hates him, intimately so. He'd like to act like that. He did, twenty-five years ago; then he became more human, less lucid, more indulgent, and today he lets the younger man become the centre of the scene, scornfully talking about a precarious job putting him in contact with average people, those who think – absurdly – that they are something.

Then the dinner is over and the moment arrives, after the goodbyes, when, looking at homes, one's own shoes or dumpsters full of glass, one realises that other people don't concern us or don't interest us. He accompanies a woman home, with whom he has a duty-free relationship. She's latching on more than they'd agreed upon, he protects himself by pretending not to understand. They fuck. A dialogue begins, where words signify something else entirely, an oblique and resentment-filled discourse that every couple knows, which I won't describe for you; it lasts for hours, while debris gathers in his mind: prisoners' uniforms, the younger man, the act of cutting, a plethora of details, on the periphery of his consciousness, which he didn't know he'd kept. He thinks of a car, an episode of his own adolescence, a word neither here nor there, like 'exanthematic' or 'organoleptic'; he thinks of plants and small animals, insects for example, of how everybody exists in a swarm and disappears unemphatically, without believing to be something. It's horrible. It's horrible but it doesn't matter.

Translation by Jacob Blakesley

Quattro superfici

Gli altri in quanto esseri esteriori,
superfici o corpi. Chi dice io invece non ha corpo,
vede soltanto le proprie mani, le guarda come pròtesi,
osserva gli altri mentre tengono la propria
vita interna dentro i volti,
scopre di avere un volto solo nelle foto.
È osceno essere esposto, essere una cosa – io, quest'auto,
la vetrina del barbiere, la busta
delle patatine sul marciapiede di via Gallia.
La seconda superficie è la percezione,
il modo in cui crea un piano di realtà semplificando.
A volte, in sogno, vedo le persone
senza la parete addominale, con gli organi aperti.
È un sogno, significa molto.
In questa poesia significa ciò che normalmente
resta impercepito, la meccanica del corpo, il tubo
di feci che portate dentro per esempio, la sorpresa
di quando la merda si mostra all'esterno come una sostanza aliena.
La terza superficie è il linguaggio,
le sue astrazioni, l'idea che *possa, esistere* e *qualcosa*
come ciò che i segni possa, esistere e qualcosa
cercano in questa frase di esprimere.
La quarta è l'immagine interna degli altri,
il loro peso immenso, il loro campo.
Agisco per voi, scrivo questa poesia per essere accolto,
divento libero solo quando morite internamente.
Il rimorchio sbanda contro la nostra auto fra Chiusi e Roma,
io lo osservo senza angoscia, è una specie
di sguardo puro, di cinematografia della mia morte. Ma Daniele
Balicco resta calmo, l'automobile passa, per qualche minuto
non parliamo, poi tornano gli aneddoti,
le biografie, quattro persone.
L'inglese ha un'espressione che mi piace molto,
small talk. Sono i discorsi di superficie,

Four Surfaces

Others, qua external beings,
surfaces or bodies. The one who says 'I' has no body,
sees only his own hands, looks at them as prostheses,
observes others as they keep their own
inner life within their faces,
discovers his own face only in photos.
It is obscene to be exposed, to be a thing – me, this car,
the barbershop window, the bag
of potato chips on the sidewalk of via Gallia.
The second surface is perception,
the way it creates a plane of reality by simplifying.
At times, in dreams, I see people
without an abdominal wall, organs exposed.
It's a dream, it means a lot.
In this poem it means what normally
remains unperceived, the body's mechanics, the tube
of faeces you carry within yourself, for example, the surprise
at how shit, on the outside, looks like an alien substance.
The third surface is language,
its abstractions, the idea that something can exist
the way the signs *something*, *can*, and *exist*
seek, in this sentence, to express.
The fourth is the inner image of others,
their immense weight, their field.
I act for you, I write this poem to be welcomed,
I become free only when you die internally.
The tow truck hits our car between Chiusi and Rome,
I observe it dispassionately, a species
of pure gaze, the cinematography of my death. But Daniele
Balicco stays calm, the car goes by, for a few minutes
we don't speak, then it all comes back, anecdotes,
biographies, four people.
The English language has an expression that I like,
'small talk'. This is surface discourse,

207

le parole di contatto, ciò che Heidegger,
in *Essere e tempo*, chiama la chiacchiera, *das Gerede*. In italiano,
nella nostra lingua interna, la parola che usiamo più spesso
per indicare tutto questo è 'cazzate'.
Le opinioni su ciò che ignoriamo, i discorsi
che escono dai cellulari e entrano nei vagoni
in mezzo a tutti: i figli, un'infezione all'unghia, la Juventus,
i nemici privati che non conosciamo – gli altri
parlano di cazzate. Chi dice io fa eccezione, è l'unico
che esista veramente, è il soggetto.
Quando Daniele Balicco riprende il controllo siamo vivi,
parliamo di cazzate. Non aderisco a nulla, mi sembra
che non aderiate a nulla, siete la parte che manca
nel vostro mondo, siete un luogo inabitato.

contact words, what Heidegger,
in *Being and Time*, calls chatter, *das Gerede*. In Italian,
in our inner tongue, the word we use most often
to indicate this is *cazzate*, 'bullshit'.
Opinions on what we know nothing about, the kind of talk
that comes out of cellphones and enters train cars
in the midst of everyone: kids, a nail infection, Juventus,
private enemies of whom we're unaware – it's others
who bullshit. The one who says 'I' is the exception, is the only one
who really exists, is the subject.
When Daniele Balicco takes control of the wheel, we're alive,
we bullshit. I adhere to nothing, it seems to me
you adhere to nothing, you're the missing part
of your world, you're the uninhabited place.

Translation by Dylan Joseph Montanari

UMBERTO PIERSANTI

Umberto Piersanti was born in Urbino in 1941. He taught sociology of literature at the University of Urbino. His books of poems include: *I luoghi persi* (Einaudi, 1994); *Nel tempo che precede* (Einaudi, 2002); *L'albero delle nebbie* (Einaudi 2008); *Nel folto dei sentieri* (Marcos y Marcos, 2015); and *Campi d'ostinato amore* (La Nave di Teseo, 2020).

Piersanti has also written four novels; *L'uomo delle cesane* (Camunia, 1994); *L'estate dell'altro millennio* (Marsilio, 2001); *Olimpo* (Avagliano, 2006); and *Cupo tempo gentile* (Marcos y Marcos, 2012). He has also published one collection of short stories, *Anime Perse* (Marcos y Marcos, 2018). Piersanti is close to the classic lyrical tradition which goes from Petrarch down to Leopardi, who was born in the same region. He is captivated by myth, nature, the past and the memory of 'lost places'.

TRANSLATOR

Matthew F. Rusnak is professor of English and Italian at Bucks County Community College in Pennsylvania. He holds a PhD in Italian from Rutgers University, where he taught for a decade. A specialist in 18th-century literature, he translated the Galateo of Giovanni Della Casa (Chicago, 2013). He divides his time between Florence and Princeton, NJ.

L'isola

Ricordi il mirto, fitto tra le boscaglie,
bianchissimo e odoroso, scendere per i dirupi
sopra quel mare? e le capre
tenaci brucare il timo, l'enigma
dello sguardo che si posa
dovunque e sempre assente?

più non so il luogo dell'imbarco
come salimmo nel battello
quali erano le carte per il viaggio.

Scendevi alta per lo stradino polveroso
antica come le ragazze
che portarono i panni alle fontane
la tua carne era bruna come la loro.

Férmati nella radura dove il vento
ha disseccato e sparso i rosmarini
qui potremmo vederle se aspettiamo
immobili alle euforbie quando imbruna
vanno alla bella fonte degli aneti
giocano lì nell'acqua e tra le erbe
e mai s'è udito un pianto
sono felici.

Tu eri come loro, solo una volta
quando uscivi dal mare, ti sei seduta
nei gradini del tempio, un'ombra appena
trascorse di dolore nella faccia.

Seppi così che il tempo era finito
che tra gli dei si vive
un giorno solo.

E riprendemmo il mare
normali rotte.

The Island

Do you recall myrtle, thick among the brush,
so white and fragrant, descending down the crags
above the sea? And the goats
fiercely grazing on thyme, the enigma
of their look directed
everywhere and always absent?

I do not know the point where we embarked
how we climbed up into the boat
what were the papers for the voyage.

You stood tall going down the dusty lane
ancient in time as the girls
that took their laundry to the fountain
your skin was brown just like theirs.

Stop yourself in the clearing where the wind
has dried out and scattered the rosemary
here we could see them if we waited long enough
quite still in the euphorbias when the sky darkens
they go to a spring there in the dill
play in the water and in the grass
and never a cry was heard
they are content.

You were the same, just one time
when coming out of the sea, you sat down to rest
on the steps of the temple, a shadow barely
moved across the suffering of your face.

I knew then that time was over and done
that among gods one lives
one day only.

And we put to sea again
on normal routes.

Qualcun altro s'imbarca, attende il turno
né l'isola sprofonda
come vorrei.

Someone else gets aboard, waits a turn
nor will the island sink
as I would like.

Translation by Matthew F. Rusnak

Lo stradino

in quale tempo
padre, il più remoto
scendevi lo stradino
sotto il Gran Masso
ed io ti stavo dietro
col ramo d'olmo,
m'arresto al cespo chiaro
che più non vedo,
il dolcino dal gambo di latte,
lo succhio contro il sole,
cola sul viso,
non c'è più stata
una luce così forte
l'erba mai più ha brillato
tanto intensa,
se le vicende restano per sempre
disegnate e sospese dentro l'aria
chiedo di rivederle una volta sola
di ritrovare ancora lo stradino
che tu dai sassi sgombri
e dagli sterpi,
ma di rado ti volgi
– verdi occhi calmi –
non cova la minaccia
dietro i monti,
la nebbia non s'addensa
il vento tace

oggi un fanciullo corre
nello spiazzo d'erba
macerata, pista margherite
fangose, di dicembre,
sale sul tronco
attonito, si torce,

The Lane

when was the time
father, long ago
when you took the lane
down under Gran Masso
and I walked behind you
with an elm branch in hand,
I pause at a bright shrub
that no one sees anymore,
the sweetness of its milky stem,
I suck against the sun,
it drips onto my face
never was there
a light so strong again
the grass never shone
so intense,
if events remain forever
designed and suspended in the air
I ask to see them only once more
to find again that little street
from which you clear pebbles
and some twigs,
but rarely you turn
– calm green eyes –
menace doesn't brood
behind the mountain,
mist doesn't thicken
wind is silent

today a little boy runs
in the space of the soaked
grass, trails of muddy
December daisies,
he gets up on a trunk
astonished, squirming,

e tra ligustri sporchi,
dei cancelli,
dove canta il fringuello
imprigionato,
entra
si perde
urla,
viene il padre
di lì lo tira fuori
lo consola,
porge le patatine
ad una ad una

e lui la vita passa
nello spiazzo,
lo stradino non c'è
da uscire fuori,
a sera, il padre
nella casa nemica l'accompagna,
lo bacia sulla porta
e poi scompare

and through messy privets,
through gates,
where finches sing
imprisoned,
he enters
gets lost
screams,
the father comes
pulls him out of there
consoles him,
gives him potato chips
one by one

and he passes his life
in open spaces,
the lane to get out,
is not there.
in the evening, the father
accompanies him to a hostile house,
kisses him at the doorstep
then disappears

Translation by Matthew F. Rusnak

La giostra

ah, quella giostra antica
nella ressa di scooter
di ragazze vocianti, luminose
dentro jeans stretti
e falsotrasandati,
dei fuoristrada rossi
sul lungomare,
escono da ogni porta,
da ogni strada,
straripano nell'aria che già avvampa,
è l'ora che precede
dolce la sera

ma nessuno che salga
sui cavalli, di legno
coi pennacchi e quella tromba
gialla, come nel libro
di letture, la musica
distante e incantata,
quella che rese altri
le zucche e i rospi

lì c'era una ragazza
tutta sola,
vestita da Pierrot
la faccia bianca,
nessuno che prendesse
i bei croccanti,
lo zucchero filato
dalla sua mano

Jacopo che tra gli altri
passa, senza guardare,
dondola il grande corpo

Carousel

that antique merry-go-round
in the crowd of scooters
the chatty girls, shining
in tight jeans
bohemian chic,
red four-wheelers
on the beachfront road,
kids exit from every door,
from every street,
they overflow into sunset flares,
it is the hour that comes before
the sweet evening

but no one gets up
on horses made of wood
with plumes and the yellow trumpet,
storybooks and music
distant and enchanting,
that transforms
pumpkins and frogs

a girl was all alone
she was dressed like Pierrot
her face white
nobody took
crunchy sugared nuts,
and cotton candy
from her hand

Jacopo passes through
the others, without looking,
sways his bulky body
and gets above them,
embraced a horse

e li sovrasta,
abbracciò un cavallo
e poi pendeva
dopo riuscì ad alzarsi,
rise forte

figlio che giri solo
nella giostra,
quegli altri la rifiutano
così antica e lenta,
ma il padre t'aspetta,
sgomento ed appartato
dietro il tronco,
che il tuo sorriso mite
t'accompagni
nel cerchio della giostra,
nella zattera dove stai
senza compagni

and then leaned
after pulling himself up,
laughed out loud

son that goes around alone
on the carousel,
others reject it
so antique and so slow,
but father waits for you
dismayed and secluded
behind a nearby tree,
your mild smile
accompanies you
in the circle of the carousel,
in the raft where you stay
without companions

Translation by Matthew F. Rusnak

Figlio per sempre

e t'avvicini,
gli scagli l'acqua addosso,
poi li guardi,
anche loro ti fissano,
sgomenti,
non sai come raggiungerli,
quel gioco funziona con tuo padre
e nessun altro,
ritorni verso il bordo,
l'acqua più fredda,
e ci sprofondi

prima mi sorridevi
sotto l'acqua,
elfo inconoscibile
e distante,
non è una cuffia quella
ma un cappuccio
che svolazza remoto
tra le bolle

io sono uscito, sai
che l'acqua mi gelava
il piede rotto,
e le mie tempie ghiacce,
fatte pietre,
tu nel gelo ci vivi
e ti ristori

quando scende lo scuro
dietro i vetri
e l'orologio brilla
contro i pini
se ne vanno i ragazzi

Son Forever

and you go closer
flinging water on them,
then look,
they stare at you as well,
dismayed,
you don't know how to reach them,
that game only works with your father
and no one else,
you return to the edge,
the water is cooler,
and you sink there

at first you were smiling
under the water,
elf unknowable
and distant,
that is no bathing cap
but a hood
that flaps remote
amidst the bubbles

I got out, you know
as the water was freezing
my broken foot,
and my icy temples,
were made stone,
you live in that chill
and restore yourself

when darkness comes
behind the windows
and the clock beams
against the pines
the kids all go away

con le borse,
tu ormai solo
nell'acqua,
con la testa all'indietro,
varchi le corde

mentre le porte chiudono,
s'accendono i soffitti
e le finestre,
inghiotti merendine
come da sempre,
o figlio che non cresci
figlio per sempre

with their bags,
you are now left alone
in the water,
with your head arched back,
you pass beyond the ropes

while the doors close up,
the ceilings alight
and the windows,
you gulp down some snacks
as always,
oh son who does not grow up
son forever

Translation by Matthew F. Rusnak

Oggi e ieri

oggi che il passo arranca
in questa età, ohimè,
non più di mezzo
che s'inoltra
ed il ginocchio gonfiatosi di notte
senza corsa o cozzo,
è solo preavviso,
nelle scalette ripide dei borghi
marchigiani aperti all'Appennino
non riesco a starti dietro
Jacopo, quando t'avventi

oggi tu di spalle
e d'altezza mi sopravanzi,
ma la tua corsa cieca
che mai si volge
e mai ritorna,
è solo più sfrenata
ma sempre quella
di te a quattr'anni
quando scendevi i campi
e come allora
figlio che non cresci
bisogna che qualcuno
ti fermi
e riaccompagni

oggi che la strada
s'è fatta
irta di buche e sassi,
a me la mente s'ostina
in altro luogo,
giorno d'autunno forse,
o primavera,

Today and Yesterday

today the step stumbles
at this age, alas,
no longer in the middle
it pushes itself forward
and my knee swells at night
without having run or fallen,
it is only noticed on the steps
of small towns in the Marche
that open to the Apennines
I cannot manage to stay behind you
Jacopo, when you speed up the pace

today you have surpassed me
at the shoulders and in height,
but your blind race
that never turns
and will never return
is only more frenetic
but always that
you ran at four-years-old
when you would go down in the field
and like back then
son that doesn't grow up
you need someone
to stop you
and accompany you once more

today that same street
is taken
rough with holes and stones,
my mind insists on
another place,
an autumn day perhaps,
or springtime,

e c'eravamo tutti,
io, te, la madre,
dentro quei lunghi vicoli
affacciati,
sopra gli orti sospesi
i tetti vasti

dopo, ti cadde
una scarpina là,
tra i coppi,
ma io la tirai su
con lunga canna,
una gran pesca
bella, miracolosa

oh, quel giovine padre
che ti solleva,
e il tuo male non c'era
ch'oggi ci schianta

and we were all there,
me, you, your mother,
within the long alleys
overlooking,
above the suspended gardens
the vast roofs

afterwards, you drop
your little shoe down there,
among the goats,
but I pull it up
with a long switch,
a great catch
gorgeous, miraculous

oh, that young father
who always lifts you up
and your sufferings were not there
that today knock us down

Translated by Matthew F. Rusnak

LAURA PUGNO

Laura Pugno was born in Rome in 1970. She writes poetry, prose, essays and plays. Pugno's poetry is like an installation where transparent and obscure objects are carefully positioned. Caught in a sort of suspended subjectivity her poetry presents elemental movements and corporeal images.

Among her latest publications are the novels *La metà di bosco* and *La ragazza selvaggia* (Marsilio, 2018 and 2016); the essay 'In territorio selvaggio. Corpo, romanzo, comunità' (Nottetempo, 2018); and the poetry collections *I diecimila giorni: poesie scelte 1991–2016* (Feltrinelli, 2016); *I legni* (Pordenonelegge/Lietocolle, 2018); and *L'alea* (Perrone, 2019).

Pugno won the Campiello Selezione Letterati Prize, the Frignano Prize for Fiction, the Dedalus and the Book of the Sea prizes. She contributes to the magazines *L'Espresso*, *Elle*, *Le parole e le cose 2*, and is one of the editors of the poetry series *I domani* published by Aragno. She was director of the Italian Cultural Institute of Madrid from 2015 to 2020.

TRANSLATOR

Craig Arnold (1967–2009) was an American poet and professor. His first book of poems, *Shells* (1999), was selected by W. S. Merwin for the Yale Series of Younger Poets. His many honours include the 2005 Joseph Brodsky Rome Prize Fellowship in literature, The Amy Lowell Poetry Traveling Fellowship, an Alfred Hodder Fellowship, a Fulbright Fellowship, an NEA fellowship, and a MacDowell Fellowship.

Vedi il suo corpo che tira di scherma

vedi il suo corpo che tira di scherma,
è nel fiume:

è in apnea e c'è una vegetazione rossa,
ora che rallenta
ogni parola e ogni lingua

tutto si muoverà allo stesso modo

hai una tuta addosso, bianca
luminescente, fa di te
qualcosa di compatto: sei un corpo
adesso più di ogni altro corpo,

hai il viso velato e le labbra perfette

e sono di nylon le pareti,
i pavimenti della stanza, ci sono
cavi per terra a forma serpentina: ci sei,
completamente c'è la tua presenza,

un corpo che si lava in una vasca rotonda, e con acqua di fiume

ripeti che la vegetazione è rossa,
che corre lungo gli argini e le pareti:
qui nel bosco,
o dominio delle piccole statue

ti metterai in ginocchio,
stella bianca,
affiora il muschio dai tagli della luce

See the body that fences

see the body that fences,
it's in the river:

it's in apnea and there's red vegetation
now that it slows down
every word and every language

all will move in the same way

you're wearing overalls, white
luminescent, you make yourself
compact: you are a body
more now than any other body,

your face veiled and your perfect lips

and the walls are nylon,
the floors of the room, there are
serpentine cables on the ground: you're there,
your presence is completely there

a body washing itself in a round tub, with river water

repeat that the vegetation's red,
that runs along the banks and walls:
here in the woods,
or the domain of little statues

you will get down on your knees,
white star,
moss emerges from the cuts of light

vedi il suo corpo, lo stesso
adesso è disarmato: il muschio è azzurro muta
tu sei pelle contro le vetrate:
qualcosa che ti copre come acqua,

visitatore,
se il tronco degli alberi ha il colore
blu delle macchine,
sei giunto

si stanno rovesciando
sott'acqua,
vasi d'elezione,
corpi di giovinezza estrema: inarca
schiena, dorso, spalle,
bianco degli occhi: si stanno
sottraendo
a questa scherma, a questa
perfezione

see the body, the same one
now disarmed: the moss is wetsuit blue
you are skin against the plate glass:
something that covers you like water,

visitor,
if the trunk of the trees is the colour
of blue cars,
you've arrived

if they are tumbling
underwater,
chosen vessels,
bodies extremely youthful: arch
your back, your spine, your shoulders,
the white of the eyes: if they are
removing themselves
from this fencing, this
perfection

Translation by Craig Arnold

Serie con kayak

kayak, è
una parola, muovi
il torso la schiena i muscoli: fai taglio
sulla superficie,
ecco, si rompe come latte

è una ragazza con la schiena dritta
orecchie piccole e bianche con orecchini di perle
non vedi le gambe –
capelli rossi incollati sulla schiena –
non vedi la sua forma di sirena,
l'acqua è immobile sotto

il kayak porta il suo corpo,
e tutto come olio

hai un salvagente sul seno e sulla schiena
tutto il tuo corpo è protetto e legato
mangi cracker
e alghe,
denti bianchissimi, non puoi fermarti:
o questo corpo muore

esci dall'acqua
tira il corpo in secca: è calda,
carne e sale,
il corpo ripete il suo cerchio
la nuca e le ginocchia,
ossa e uova

prendi un pezzo di pane come piatto
ti pulisci la bocca con mollica di pane

Kayak series

kayak, is
a word, move
the torso the back the muscles: make a cut
on the surface,
there, it breaks like milk

is a girl with a straight back
small white ears with pearl earrings
you don't see her legs –
red hair glued to her back –
you don't see her mermaid shape,
the water is motionless beneath

the kayak carries her body,
it's all like oil

you have a life jacket over breast and back
all your body is protected and fastened
you eat crackers
and algae,
the whitest teeth, you can't stop:
or this body will die

get out of the water
dry your body off: it's warm,
meat and salt,
the body repeats its rounds,
nape and knees,
bones and eggs

take a piece of bread like a plate
wipe off your mouth with breadcrumbs

torni a casa,
pane e latte, ora scrivi
la parola kayak perfettamente,
non vedi,
pane, latte e alghe

con la neve, si scioglierà come neve

you go home,
bread and milk, now write
the word kayak perfectly,
don't you see,
bread, milk and algae

with the snow, it will melt like snow

Translation by Craig Arnold

Non è la stessa lingua che parli

non è la stessa lingua che parli
se il tuo corpo è il sole,

viene perimetrato sempre lo stesso terreno,
pochi metri di ghiaccio con oasi,
una stoffa arancio
intenso su un tappeto:

una lingua, se verrà inventata

oppure, un asciugamano rosso
cupo, che ti copre la testa:
questa è la metratura
del deserto:

di notte sogni di percorrere un territorio al buio,
con una benda azzurra
intorno ai polsi, e sale
azzurro sulla bocca e sulla schiena

It's not the same language that you speak

it's not the same language that you speak
if your body is the sun,

always the same terrain is bounded,
a few metres of ice with an oasis,
orange cloth
bright on a carpet:

a language, if it gets invented

or rather, a dark red
towel that covers your head:
this is the measurement
of the desert:

at night you dream of covering territory in the dark
with a blue bandage
around your wrists, and blue
salt on your mouth and on your back

Translation by Craig Arnold

Più avanti, se la lingua è condivisa

più avanti, se la lingua è condivisa, quella
che è sul tappeto,
la luce intermittente:

entra nel leopardo, metti
le mani dentro la scultura – sabbia
di questo giardino,
sassi bianchi,

che hanno un numero o un nome

mettiti una pelliccia di plastica,
i tuoi occhi color leopardo,
gli stessi
di ieri notte, vedranno al buio

oppure entra nel lupo,
il verde che gli si fa intorno
sempre più stringendosi, il punto
esatto dove la luce filtra sul lago

Further on, if the language is shared

further on, if the language is shared, that
which is on the carpet,
the intermittent light:

enter the leopard, put
your hands inside the sculpture – sand
from this garden,
white stones,

that have a number or a name

put on a plastic pelt,
your leopard-coloured eyes,
the same
as last night, will see in the dark

or else enter the wolf,
the green that surrounds it
drawing ever tighter, the exact
point where the light filters over the lake

Translation by Craig Arnold

Apri la scatola nera

apri la scatola nera,
contiene carne
proibita, di tartaruga, di delfino:
è questo che mangiano da quando
è venuto il regno,
da questa luminescenza è invaso il reef:

se ora è l'ora della luce,
splenderai,

copriti i muscoli d'olio
davanti a te per terra
c'è una stoffa leggera come l'oro
te la potresti gettare sulle spalle

Open the black box

open the black box,
it contains forbidden
meat, turtle, dolphin:
this is what they eat since
the kingdom came,
the reef was invaded by this luminescence

if now is the hour of light,
you will shine,

cover your muscles with oil
in front of you on the ground
there's a cloth light like gold
you could throw over your shoulders

Translation by Craig Arnold

IDA TRAVI

Ida Travi was born in Cologne, Brescia, in 1948. In 2000 she published the essays *L'aspetto orale della poesia* (Moretti & Vitali, 2007) and *Poetica del basso continuo* (Moretti & Vitali, 2015).

Travi's poetry deals with the volatile and unexpressed relationship between spoken language and writing. She created a world populated by people called Tolki (a word derived from the English verb to talk) who are very much like us. Inna, Usov, Zet, Katrin, Sasa, Olin, Dora Pal, Van, Sunta, Kraus and the others are (human) beings marked by language, sacred and miserable, mysterious and simple. There are five poetry collections about the Tolki all published by Moretti & Vitali: *TA'poesia dello spiraglio e della neve* (2011); *Il mio nome è Inna* (2012); *Katrin, Saluti dalla casa di nessuno* (2015); *Dora Pal, la terra* (2017); and *Tasàr, animale sotto la neve* (2018).

Some of Travi's radio plays and poetry have had musical scores composed for them by contemporary musicians, and she has collaborated with the American composer, Scott Wheeler. She has taken part in numerous national and international festivals and her work has been translated into English, Greek, Spanish, French, German and Russian.

TRANSLATORS

Tommaso Jacopo Gorla is a researcher, editor and translator from Verona, Italy. He holds a PhD in Cultural Anthropology from EHESS, Paris and is chief editor of the visual culture journal *Anima Loci*. He currently teaches Critical and Contextual Studies at London Metropolitan University.

Alexandra Wilk works as an independent researcher and designer. She is a co-founder and editor of the online visual culture journal *Anima Loci*. Alex lives between London and Verona and holds an MA in Cultural Studies from Goldsmiths, University of London.

Il nome Tasàr è riferimento e omaggio all'asino Balthazar, figura centrale nel film Au hasard Balthazar di Robert Bresson (1966). A tratti in questo libro, c'è la traccia trasfigurata di quell'animale, del suo nome, così come suonerebbe nella pronuncia dei Tolki, così come è scritto: Tasàr. I nomi degli esseri umani che compaiono in questo libro sono nomi d'invenzione.

Chi sono i Tolki

Esseri sacri e miserabili, misteriosi e semplici.
Penso a un Tolki come a un *parlêtre,*
un essere marchiato dal linguaggio. *Parlêtre* è un neologismo di Lacan
che fonde l'essere al linguaggio, nell'atto della pronuncia.
Il *parlêtre* rompe con la tradizione della metafisica intenta
a 'pensare l'essere': vedo i Tolki come *lavoranti o non lavaranti,*
esseri che nello scontro con la poesia assumono su se stessi il peso
d'un linguaggio povero, duro come una colpa,
leggero come una liberazione.

(il bambino e l'animale)

Il bambino e l'animale
sembrano fratelli, sono uguali
aspettano così tranquilli

Li chiamo, e non girano la testa
sono d'oro, sono nel tempo d'oro
io non li stacco dalla loro eternità

Dovrebbero farci scuola, dovrebbero
dirci cosa c'è nell'oro
perché io l'ho perduto l'anello
e tu?

The name Tasàr is a reference and tribute to Balthazar the donkey, a central figure in the film Au hasard Balthazar *by Robert Bresson (1966). In this book, there is the transformed trace of that animal, of its name, as it would sound in the Tolki pronunciation, as it is written: Tasàr. The names of human beings that appear in this book are invented.*

Who are the Tolki?

Beings who are sacred and miserable, mysterious and simple.
I consider a Tolki as a *parlêtre*,
a being branded by language. *Parlêtre* is a neologism by Lacan
that fuses being with language, in the act of pronunciation.
The *parlêtre* breaks with the metaphysical tradition, intent
on 'reflecting on being': I see the Tolki as *workers or non-workers*,
beings that in the collision with poetry assume the weight
of a poor language, as hard as guilt,
light as liberation.

(the child and the animal)

The child and the animal
look like brothers, they're identical
waiting so calmly

I call them, and they don't turn around
they're golden, they're in golden time
I don't remove them from their eternity

They should teach us, they should
tell us what's in the gold
because I lost the ring
and you?

Translation by Alexandra Wilk and Tommaso Gorla

251

(il muso)

Il muso lo puoi toccare
ma resta lontano dagli zoccoli

Se devi raccogliere la chiave
mettiti davanti, se sei triste
aspetta che sia buio, e lì
con la coperta sulla testa
troverai la fratellanza

Troverai la chiave, Antòn
troverai il carretto
andrai per questa terra

Troverai la vipera
e il sasso sotto la ruota
sarai felice, e in tasca
avrai per sempre il verme
la formica.

(the snout)

The snout you can touch
but stay away from the hooves

If you need to collect the key
put yourself forward, if you're sad
wait until it's dark, and there
with the blanket on your head
you'll find brotherhood

You'll find the key, Antòn
you'll find the cart
you'll go through this land

You'll find the viper
and the stone under the wheel
you'll be happy, and in your pocket
you'll always have the worm
the ant.

Translation by Alexandra Wilk and Tommaso Gorla

(lo schermo parla chiaro)

Lo schermo parla chiaro
il secchio, il legno, il recinto
tutto parla chiaro: ogni cosa
porta in fronte il suo sigillo

– Tasàr! –

Ve lo dico per l'ultima volta
ogni cosa vi saluta
e voi rispondete, rispondete
non dovete credere
di essere chissà chi.

(the screen speaks clearly)

The screen speaks clearly
the bucket, the wood, the fence
everything speaks clearly: every thing
bears its mark on its forehead

– Tasàr! –

I'll tell you this for the last time
every thing greets you
and you shall respond, you respond
don't believe
that you're all that.

Translation by Alexandra Wilk and Tommaso Gorla

(l'animale)

L'animale è sacro, non dovete
trattarlo così. Non lo vedete il lampo?
Il diluvio sta per venire
Ed è per cattiveria, è solo
per la vostra cattiveria

Ha due occhi, come voi
ha il naso come voi, come voi
quando portavate gli zoccoli

Ha la fronte, come voi, e dietro
la fronte si stende il cielo nero

E le nuvole, e il volo degli uccelli
e l'amore che arriva di notte
l'amore che arriva di notte
e si siede sulla branda
non appena si spegne la luce

Non appena si spegne la luce
come voi, come voi, Tasàr
Tasàr, è con voi, nelle tenebre.

(the animal)

The animal is sacred, you shouldn't
treat it like that. Don't you see the lightning?
The downpour is coming
And it's out of spite, it's only
for your spite

He has two eyes, like you
He has a nose like you, like you
when you wore the clogs

He has a brow, like you, and behind
the brow the black sky spreads out

And the clouds, and the flight of the birds
and the love that arrives by night
the love that arrives by night
and that sits on the camp bed
as soon as the light goes out

As soon as the light goes out
like you, like you, Tasàr
Tasàr, is with you, in the darkness.

Translation by Alexandra Wilk and Tommaso Gorla

(presto)

Presto ce ne andremo sul monte
ce ne andremo, in groppa a Tasàr

Volevamo il comando
volevamo fare i padroni
e invece...

Avremo una casa, Kraus
anche noi, anche noi

Saliremo sul monte
la neve sopra di noi
l'asino sotto di noi
e intorno le volpi
gli angeli, gli spiriti, i villaggi.

(soon)

Soon we'll go to the mount
we'll go there, on the back of Tasàr

We wanted to command
we wanted to be the masters
and instead...

We'll have a house, Kraus
us too, us too

We'll climb the mount
the snow on top of us
the donkey below us
and all around the foxes
the angels, the spirits, the villages.

Translated by Alexandra Wilk and Tommaso Gorla

LUIGI TRUCILLO

Luigi Trucillo was born in Naples in 1955, where he lives and works today. Trucillo has published seven books of poetry: *Navicelle*, with a preface by the philosopher Giorgio Agamben (Cronopio, 1995); *Carta Mediterranea* (Donzelli, 1997); *Polveri* (Cronopio, 1998); *Le Amorose* (Quodlibet, 2004); *Lezioni di tenebra*, winner of the Lorenzo Montano Prize 2008 (Cronopio, 2007); *Darwin*, winner of the Naples Prize 2009 (Quodlibet, 2009); and *Altre amorose* (Quodlibet, 2017). In his poetry there is an expressive contraction in which daily objects and thoughts are inextricably linked.

Trucillo's novel, *Quello che ti dice il fuoco* (Mondadori, 2013), was later translated into German with the title *Die Geometrie der Liebe* (Mareverlag, 2015) He also adapted *The Magic Flute* for the Neapolitan Piazza Vittorio's Orchestra. He has written for the literary magazines *Paragone* and *Nuovi Argomenti* and collaborated with the cultural page of *Il Manifesto*.

TRANSLATORS

Martin Corless-Smith was born and raised in Worcestershire. He is the author of a dozen books, most recently *The Melancholy of Anatomy* (Shearsman Books, 2021). His other translations include Horace, Verlaine and Giovanna Marmo. He directs the MFA program in Creative Writing at Boise State University, in Idaho, USA.

Patricio Ferrari is a poet, editor, and literary translator (English, Spanish, Portuguese, French, and Italian). He is responsible for seven Pessoa editions, including the first critical edition of his *Poèmes français* (Éditions de la Différence, 2014). He teaches at Rutgers University in New Jersey and is Managing Director of San Patricio Language Institute.

James Schwarten received his PhD in Italian from the University of Wisconsin, Madison, USA. His interests include sociology, anthropology, translation, and literature. He is currently an adjunct professor with several universities in Rome and a regular translator for John Cabot University's ongoing Italian poetry anthology *InVerse*. In 2015, he translated Dacia Maraini's theatrical pieces (*Extravagance* and *Three Other Plays*, Rowman and Littlefield, ed.).

Lamiere

Lamiere:
sono la prima preghiera
di Efesto
al lontano balenare
dei fichi,
l'amarezza degli occhi
che si torce smarrita
in queste tenebre.
Ci sono alghe
che ci dormono a fianco
e rupi, e tuoni:
basta vederli
scardinare le gabbie
con passo sordo
prima di trasformarsi
in fantasmi.
E ci sono coltelli
anche dopo la morte
quando l'orizzonte
non ha più vulcani
dove accendersi.
Col dito segno
un tracciato d'oro
nelle nubi di polvere:
da qui i confini non scritti
del fuoco
ricorderanno il mondo
senza difendersi,
rammenteranno l'asse del sole
e il bianco lino
con cui la vita si fasciava
come una vergine.
Da qui si curverà
docile

Sheets

Sheets:
they are the first prayer
of Hephaestus
far away flash
of figs,
the bitterness of eyes
that twists lost
in this darkness.
There are algae
that sleep next to us
and cliffs, and thunders:
just see them
unhinge the cages
with dull pace
before turning
into phantoms.
And there are knives
even after death
when the horizon
has no more volcanoes
where to ignite.
With the finger sign
a path of gold
in dust clouds:
from here the unwritten boundaries
of fire
will remember the world
without defending themselves,
they will remember the axis of the sun
and the white linen
with which life bandaged
like a virgin.
From here it will bend
docile

il passato
a mangiarci nel grembo,
e i volti degli uccisi
rifioriranno lenti
come bulbi dorati.
Da qui, da qui
le nostre mani si lasceranno
come un rintocco che scuote
ancora un giorno,
ancora un colpo,
sul petto,
il taciturno.

the past
to eat us in the womb,
and the faces of the slain
they will return lenses
as golden bulbs.
From here, from here
our hands will leave
like a toll that shakes
one more day,
one more shot,
on the chest,
the taciturn.

Translation by Martin Corless-Smith and Patricio Ferrari

The tube

Ciò che ci fu dato
è un sentiero
che diventò un villaggio,
e siccome le ore
si trasformavano in ruggine
i mostri divennero piogge
e le stazioni muschi.
A luglio andammo,
a marzo
macchiandoci di onde.
Di sosta in sosta
demmo quiete
al lutto di Demetra
versando luci e oro
come offerta;
felici,
come può esserlo un demente,
perché il regno dell'aria
senza di noi
era un campo di locuste.
O corpo, lingua, sole,
unica cura
per chi già dorme!
'Risaliranno nel mondo
a cercare l'equilibrio
– mormoravano i vecchi –
Scinderanno l'oro
dal fango
aspirando il ramo
di menta
a primavera.
E capiranno
che ogni madre lontana
è una cicala,

The tube

What was given to us
it is a path
which became a village,
and as the hours
turned into rust
monsters became rains
and stations musk.
In July we went,
in March
staining with waves.
Stopover
we were quiet
to the mourning of Demeter
pouring lights and gold
as an offer;
happy,
as a demented man can be,
because the kingdom of the air
without us
was a field of locusts.
O body, tongue, sun,
only care
for those asleep!
'They will go back into the world
to seek balance
– the old men murmured –
they will cut gold
from the mud
aspirating the branch
of mint
in spring.
And they will understand
that every distant mother
is a cicada,

un bianco germoglio
del sole
che concepisce un inno
dell'estate'.
Ma non capimmo
e neppure ritornammo.
E ora nei tunnel
scompaiono I vecchi,
dissipano il proprio lentissimo
sigillo
proprio come dei perpetui
passeggeri.

a white sprout
of sun
conceives a hymn
of summer.'
But we did not understand
and we did not even go back.
And now in the tunnels
the old ones disappear,
they dissipate their very slow
seal
just like perpetual
passengers.

Translation by Martin Corless-Smith and Patricio Ferrari

Casa estrema

Quando la chiave gira
una casa estrema
è quella dove i metri quadri
diventano rotondi
per esorcizzare l'incantesimo
di chi è incatenato al proprio essere.
Io sento molti lupi, e tuoni, e orsi
che nuotano nelle arterie del cemento
per smantellare la torba della mente.
Sento che la prospettiva è una balena
che ha inghiottito la libertà di Giona
esplosa nella torcia delle stelle
come se ogni falena fosse unica.
E soprattutto sento che il velo segreto
del soffitto sulla testa
nasce dalla tua gonna appesa sulla gruccia,
mattoni, malta e intonaco
con cui una mano gigantesca
puntella gli squarci vuoti del mio cuore,
quando il tuo corpo nevica,
e ovunque fiocca una cascata calda.

Extreme Home

When the key turns
an extreme house
is the one where the square metres
become round
to exorcise the spell
of one who is chained to his own being.
I hear many wolves, and thunderclaps, and bears
that swim in the arteries of the cement
to dismantle the peat of the mind.
I sense that perspective is a whale
that swallowed Jonah's freedom
exploded in the torch of the stars
as if every moth were unique.
And above all I sense that the secret veil
of the attic on my head
is born of your skirt hung on the hanger,
bricks, mortar and plaster
with which a gigantic hand
underpins the empty gashes of my heart,
when your body snows,
and everywhere a warm cascade flurries.

Translation by James Schwarten

Per Ethel Rosenberg, presunta spia comunista

Un mese prima della sedia elettrica
scrisse ai suoi figli
di un grande merlo dalle ali rosse
piombato nel patio del penitenziario
a rubare le briciole che gettava ai passeri,
e di come la scia del suo splendore
le avesse fatto sentire sulla pelle
per un attimo lentissimo
il tepore irradiante dei loro abbracci.
Poi al fruscio di un piede sulla ghiaia
il merlo volò via
trascinando con sé le loro immagini
nell'impennata di tutto ciò che è luce,
e io ora mi domando
se quei passeri attorno a lei così famelici
non erano le strane idee per cui viviamo
e vortichiamo
fino alla morte
smarriti come briciole di pane.

For Ethel Rosenberg, presumed to be a Communist Spy

A month before the electric chair
she wrote to her children
about a large blackbird with red wings that
landed in the patio of the penitentiary
to steal the crumbs that she was throwing to the sparrows,
and how the wake of its splendour
had made her feel upon her skin
for a long instant
the radiant warmth of their embraces.
Then at the swooshing of a foot on the gravel
the blackbird flew away
sweeping away their images
in the flight of all that is light,
and now I wonder
if those sparrows around her so hungry
weren't the strange ideas for which we live
and whirl
until death
lost like crumbs of bread.

Translated by James Schwarten

Giorni e luce

È ancora presto.
Lasciami prendere quello che mi hai dato
senza saperlo,
come un fiocco di neve smemorato
che costruisce il suo pupazzo
restando una danza di cristallo.
La luce ti si versa sopra il collo
a lente losanghe refluite,
e io penso che di tanto in tanto
il tocco esperto del mattino
vale lo sforzo.

Days and Light

It's still early.
Let me take what you gave me
without knowing,
like a forgetful snowflake
that builds its snowman
while remaining a crystal dance.
Light pours down above your neck
with slow diamond shapes returning,
and I think every now and then that
the expert touch of the morning
is worth the effort.

Translation by James Schwarten

PATRIZIA VALDUGA

Patrizia Valduga, poet and translator, was born in 1953 in Castelfranco Veneto, near Treviso, and lives in Milan. She studied medicine for two years, then changed to literature and philosophy. She founded the monthly magazine *Poesia* in 1988, which she edited for a year.

Her poetry explores the connection between the body and writing, using traditional metric forms (sonnet, quatrains, madrigals, syllable lines, octaves, and Dante's tercets) as a sort of anti-lyrical self-analysis. Valduga's poetry collections include: *Medicamenta* (Guanda, 1982); *La tentazione* (Crocetti, 1985); *Medicamenta e altri medicamenta* (Einaudi, 1989); *Donna di dolori* (Mondadori, 1991); *Requiem* (Marsilio, 1994); *Cento quartine e altre storie d'amore* (Einaudi, 1997); *Prima antologia* (Einaudi, 1998); *Quartine: Seconda centuria*, (Einaudi, 2001); *Afterword to Last Verses* by Giovanni Raboni (Garzanti, 2006); *Book of Lauds* (Einaudi, 2012); and *Belluno Andantino e grande fuga* (Einaudi, 2019).

She has translated several poets, including Donne, Mallarmé, Shakespeare, Kantor, Valéry, and Beckett. Valduga also published *Italiani, apprendate l'italiano!* (Edizioni d'If, 2010, new edition 2016); *Poeti innamorati* (Interlinea, 2011); *Breviario proustiano* (Einaudi, 2011); and *Per sguardi e per parole* (Il Mulino, 2018).

TRANSLATOR

Geoffrey Brock is the author of three books of poetry, the editor of *The FSG Book of Twentieth-Century Italian Poetry*, and the translator of various books, most recently Giovanni Pascoli's *Last Dream* and Giuseppe Ungaretti's *Allegria*. He teaches at the University of Arkansas.

Sonetti

8

Ora lo sai: ho bisogno di parole.
Devi imparare a amarmi a modo mio.
È la mente malata che lo vuole:
parla, ti prego! parla, Cristoddio!

17

Fa' presto, immobilizzami le braccia,
crocefiggimi, inchiodami al tuo letto;
consolami, accarezzami la faccia;
scopami quando meno me l'aspetto.

45

Da nervi vene valvole ventricoli
da tendini da nervi e cartilagini
papille nervi costole clavicole…
in spasmi da ogni poro mi esce l'anima.

47

Allora ce l'hai fatta? sei venuta?
e come sei venuta? dimmi. Prego?
Se ti è piaciuto molto sei perduta.
Non lo posso negare e non lo nego.

71

Perché anche il piacere è come un peso
e la mente che è qui mi va anche via?
Su, spiegamelo tu. *Per chi mi hai preso?*
per un docente di filosofia?

Sonnets

8

By now you know: I need the words.
You'll have to learn the right technique.
It's my sick mind, it feeds on words.
I'm begging you, for God's sake: speak!

17

Hurry, pin my wrists in place,
nail me to your bed like Christ...
comfort me, caress my face...
fuck me when I expect it least.

45

From nerves veins valves ventricles
from tendons cartilage nerves ducts
from follicles nerves ribs clavicles...
from every pore my soul erupts.

47

You liked that? you actually came?
but how? Explain to me. But why?
If you got off on that, you're doomed.
A charge I can't and don't deny.

71

Why is even pleasure a kind of chore?
Why is what sense I have left leaving me?
Come on, explain. *Who do you take me for,*
your personal doctor of philosophy?

Translation by Geoffrey Brock

Sonetti

107

Io sono sempre stata come sono
anche quando non ero come sono
e non saprà nessuno come sono
perché non sono solo come sono.

122

Lui o un altro che differenza fa
se poi ho da sentirmi sempre sola?
Solo con la mia moribilità…
se esistesse questa bella parola…

124

Ho le emorroidi: sangue anche di lì…
rotta in culo… per dirla in stile aulico…
Perdo da tutti i buchi… tutti… sì:
ci sarebbe bisogno di un idraulico.

154

Vuoi morire con me, testa di cazzo?
Scavare nel mio cuore con la vanga?
Si sta prendendo proprio un bell'andazzo…
Vuoi che giuri in ginocchio? Vuoi che pianga?

Sonnets

107

I have always been the way I am
even when I wasn't the way I am
and none can ever know the way I am
because I am not merely the way I am

122

Him or someone else, what's it to me
if every time I'm lonely afterward?
Alone here with my moribility...
if there only were such a lovely word...

124

These haemorrhoids, this bleeding from behind...
I'm spilling out of all my holes – yes, all.
My arse is wrecked... (My speech is so refined...)
There ought to be a plumber I could call.

154

You want to die with me, you dumb shit?
Excavate my heart with your shovel?
This is getting to be a hell of a habit.
Want me to swear on my knees? Grovel?

Translation by Geoffrey Brock

GIOVANNA CRISTINA VIVINETTO

Giovanna Cristina Vivinetto was born in Siracusa, Sicily in 1994, and currently lives in Rome, where she is studying Modern Philology after graduating in Modern Literature at La Sapienza University.

Dolore Minimo (Interlinea, 2018); is the first collection of Italian poetry to address the subject of transsexuality and gender dysphoria. With an introduction by Dacia Maraini and an afterword by Alessandro Fo, the book was featured in Italy's major newspapers and won several prizes, including the Viareggio Opera Prima in 2019 for best debut. In 2020, BUR Rizzoli published Vivinetto's second book of poems, *Dove non siamo stati.*

TRANSLATOR

Cristina Viti is a translator and poet working with Italian, English and French. Recent translations include Anna Gréki's *The Streets of Algiers* (Smokestack Books, 2020); Mariangela Gualtieri's *Beast of Joy* (Chelsea Editions, 2018); and Elsa Morante's *The World Saved by Kids* (Seagull Books, 2016), shortlisted for the John Florio Prize.

***

La prima perdita furono le mani.
Mi lasciò il tocco ingenuo
che si addentrava nelle cose, le scopriva
con piglio bambino – le plasmava
Erano mani che non sapevano
ritrarsi: mani di dodici anni
mani di figli che tendono al cono
di luce – che non sanno ancora
giungersi in preghiera.
Mani profonde – come laghi
in cui nessuno verrebbe a cercare,
mani silenti come vecchi scrigni
chiusi – mani inviolate.

La prima scoperta furono le mani.
Ricevetti un tocco adulto che sa
esattamente dove posarsi – mani
ampie e concave di una madre
che si accosta alla soglia ad aspettare;
mani di legno e di fiori
di ciliegio – mani che rinascono.
Mani che sanno aggrapparsi anche
all'esatta consistenza del nulla.

***

The first loss was the hands.
I lost the innocent touch
that delved into things, discovered them
with a child's pluck – formed them.
Hands that did not know
how to retreat: twelve-year-old hands,
children's hands reaching out for
the cone of light – that do not yet
know how to join in prayer.
Deep hands – like lakes
no one would come to fathom,
silent hands like old
locked caskets – hands untouched.
The first discovery was the hands.
I received the adult touch that knows
exactly where to land – hands
wide & cupped, hands of a mother
who moves near the threshold to wait;
hands of wood &
cherry blossom – hands being reborn.
Hands that also know how to take hold
of the exact texture of nothingness.

Translation by Cristina Viti

***

La seconda perdita fu la luce.
La malattia mi tolse la vista
dei campi abbacinati dal sole,
la trama arsa e viva dei litorali
siciliani dei miei tredici anni.
Passai quegli anni tra i fili
di panni stesi divorati dal sole,
vasi sbriciolati di terracotta
dove steli di basilico e lavanda
si inerpicavano verso la linea
del cielo – quasi a raggiungerla,
a toccarla. La luce era tutto.

La seconda scoperta fu la luce.
Non la luce che accende i terrazzi
né quella che assottiglia le strisce
di costa, ma la luce delle case
al tramonto – che si mischia all'ombra,
la luce setacciata dall'intreccio
dei rami e quella che si schiarisce
a fatica dopo un temporale
– dopo un grave malanno.
Conquistai la luce intatta dei corpi vergini –
delle fonti d'acqua
perenni che nessuno sa.

***

The second loss was the light.
The sickness stripped me of the sight
of sun-dazed fields,
scorched live weft of the shorelines
in the Sicily of my early teens.
I spent those years between the lines
of washing hung out & devoured by the sun,
crumbling earthenware
and stems of spike lavender & basil
straggling towards the skyline
– as if to reach it,
touch it. The light was everything.

The second discovery was the light.
Not the light setting terraces ablaze
or the one shimmering the strips
of coastline thin, but the light of
houses at sunset – mixing with shadow,
the light sieved through the weave
of branches & the one working
its way to clear brightness after a storm –
after harsh illness.
I conquered the intact light of virgin
bodies – of the perennial water
springs unknown to all.

Translated by Cristina Viti

***

La terza perdita fu il perdono.
Avrei voluto scusarmi per i toni
accesi verso il tuo non comprendere,
la rara gentilezza dei miei
quattordici anni quando parlavi
senza premesse. Ma la colpa
non era di nessuno: non era tua
che mi indicavi il corpo e mi dicevi
di stare attenta, che non sarebbe stato
facile – non era mia che non riuscivo
a perdonare il tuo insinuarti
maternamente tra pelle e nervi
a scovare tutte le incertezze, gli stalli
che a quel tempo non avevo.

La terza scoperta fu il perdono.
Quando fui grande abbastanza
per capire cosa volesse dire
essere madre, un perdono tondo
e commosso provai per te, e provai
per le altre donne-bambine come me
e lo provai per me, che tenevo
fino a quel punto il filo rosso dell'infanzia
e da un giorno all'altro, adultamente,
non tenevo più.

***

The third loss was forgiveness.
I would have wanted to offer an apology
for my heated tones against your failure to understand,
my scant kindness when at
fourteen I heard you speak
with no preambles. But the fault
lay with neither of us: not you
pointing at my body and saying
I must be careful, it would not be
easy – not me who failed
to forgive your sliding in
between skin & nerves, maternally
feeling for the uncertainties & deadlocks
I did not have back then.

The third discovery was forgiveness.
When I was old enough
to know what it means
to be a mother, it was a rounded
wholehearted forgiveness I felt for you,
felt for the other woman-children like me
felt for myself, who up to that point had held
the red thread of childhood
then overnight, adult-like,
stopped holding.

Translation by Cristina Viti

***

Accadde che le ombre della mia infanzia
si addensassero attorno al mio letto,
afferrandomi le caviglie, facendosi
strada sulle gambe, scivolando sul ventre,
intrecciandosi infine sul petto.

Si dice che le anime orfane
vaghino di notte in cerca delle anime
madri – a cui riallacciarsi.
Ma le ombre che sostano sui muri
sono abbagli di morte imprevisti
– ti si incurvano addosso
a bisbigliare la morte di un caro.

A quel tempo non mancò nessuno
– eppure le ombre continuavano
a rantolare una perdita.
Fu allora che compresi tutto.

Bisognava che io morissi
per strappare il mio tempo
fermo dai cespugli dell'infanzia
– che lo lasciassi riprendere
anche senza di me.

Bisognava che affidassi il mio nome
agli spiriti bambini del passato
per lasciare il posto ad altri cespugli,
ad altre infanzie, senza ombre.

***

It happened that the shadows of my childhood
would cluster thick around my bed,
gripping my ankles, making
their way along my legs, sliding over my belly,
finally interweaving across my chest.

It's said that orphaned souls
roam the night in search of souls
– mother souls to be rejoined with.
But the shadows lingering on the walls
are unforeseen flashes of death
– they bend into you
& whisper news of a loved one's death.

Back then no one had passed away
– yet the shadows would not stop
their death rattle of loss.
It was then I fully understood.

It was I needed to die
so as to tear my own
stilled time loose from the shrubs of childhood
– letting it resume
with or without me.

It was I needed to entrust my name
to the child spirits of the past
so as to make way for other shrubs,
other childhoods, free of shadows.

Translation by Cristina Viti

***

Non ho ferite che appaiono. I miei
dilemmi sono annidati ben oltre la carne.
Eppure chi mi definisce addita
il corpo come sola dimensione possibile.
Come se la colpa fosse tutta
tra le gambe o nel tono della voce,
in un cromosoma destinato
a dover restare tale e quale.
Risulta più difficile scovare
le menomazioni della mente,
determinare con esattezza
le idee che regolano l'identità,
l'umore, l'amore che ci tiene in piedi.
Ma il corpo non mente: non nega
la sua terrosa concretezza,
non allude, non travisa, c'è
e si espone, materializza.
Il corpo è solo, perciò è esatto,
circostanziato, dunque corruttibile.
E questa è sua debolezza
e sua corticale potenza.
Assediata, piegata, avvilita
è l'unica forma sana che mi rimane.

***

I've no visible wounds. My
dilemmas are nestled well beyond the flesh.
Yet those who would define me point their finger
at the body as the sole possible dimension.
As if the fault lay entirely
between the legs or in the voice's timbre,
in a chromosome destined
to remain ever equal to itself.
It proves more difficult to uncover
where the mind's wanting,
to exactly determine
which ideas govern identity,
mood, or the love keeps us standing.
But the body won't lie, won't deny
its own earthy concreteness,
won't allude or misconstrue, it is there
it exposes itself, gives material substance.
The body is alone and therefore exact,
circumstantial, hence corruptible.
Therein lies its flaw
and its cortical power.
Besieged, subdued, cast down
is the only whole form I have left.

Translation by Cristina Viti

LELLO VOCE

Lello Voce is a poet and performer. He is one of the pioneers of spoken word and spoken music in Europe and introduced the poetry slam to Italy. He has published several books and CDs of poetry, with artists such as Fresu, Nemola, Salis, De Vito, Gross and Merlino including *Farfalle da combattimento* (Bompiani, 1999); *Fast Blood* with illustrations by Sandro Chia (2003, winner of the Delfini Prize for Poetry); *L'esercizio della lingua* (Le Lettere, 2010); and *Piccola cucina cannibale* with Nemola and Calia (Squi[libri], 2011), for which he was awarded the Premio Napoli 2012.

His latest CD-book, again with Frank Nemola and featuring Paolo Fresu, is *Il fiore inverso* (Squi[libri], 2016), for which he was awarded the Elio Pagliarani National Prize for Poetry 2016. Since 2017, he has been the chief editor of *Canzoniere*, a series of books and CDs dedicated to poetry with music and poetry comics, with Squi[libri].

TRANSLATOR

Susanna Maggioni is a translator and reviewer with a background in the performing arts. A certified nature guide specialised in bike touring, she's also an environmentalist and the chair of the Treviso cycling association. Her translation works include graphic novels, such as *Silk road to ruin* by Ted Rall, and *King* by Ho-Che Anderson, as well as memoirs, autobiographies, and children's books on Venice.

Lai del ragionare lento

Così non va, non va, non va, ti dico
           che così non va: come una supernova
esplosa come un astro strizzato di fresco
                    come la tua bocca stanca e tesa
accelerata come particella ora non so più
                    nemmeno se sia una stella o invece
pajette incollata allo sguardo scheggia
                    di diamante che ti fora le pupille o
desiderio di luce che sfarfalla all'orizzonte
                    dell'ultimo oltremondo viaggio
condanna che ci danna panna acida che
                    ingozza la parola che ora già ci strozza
perché così non va, non va, non va:
           è ormai soltanto un buco nero di sentimenti
e fiati amore addomesticato casalingo come
                    un tigre prigioniero o invece credi
che dovremmo dimissionare l'anima e
                    restar lì a vedere se alla fine ci sarà il
premio il lingotto la crociera che ci crocifigge
                    lo sforzo che infine ci infigge nel
ricordo lo *share* di un suicidio spettacolare
                    e notiziabile sintesi ultima dello scibile
di noi genere umano di noi genere estinto
                    di noi umani generati usati rottamati

(se ti parlo ormai non mi parlo, se mi parlo
           ormai non ti parlo e se ne parlo credimi
è solo perché nel fiato che si elide in pensieri
           resta la nostalgia di quando era ieri)

Così non dura, non dura, non dura, vi dico
           che così non dura: qui si muore di fame
e d'obesità si muore di ricchezza e povertà,
           si muore di solitudine e rumore si muore

296

Lai of Reasoning Slowly

That's not good so, not good, not good, I tell you
                              that's not good so: like a supernova
gushing forth like a freshly squeezed planet
                              like your mouth tired and taut
like a smashed particle now I no longer even know
                              whether it's an astral jewel or
rather a sequin glued to your gaze diamond shard
                              piercing your pupils or
yearning for light flickering at the horizon
                              of the last netherworld journey
we're doomed and can't be redeemed sour cream
                              stuffing the word already choking us
because that's not good, not good, not good so:
                              now nothing but a black hole of feelings
and breaths tamed homemaker love like
                              a captive tiger or would you rather say
that we should dismiss the soul and
                              stay there and see whether at the end there shall be
the prize the ingot the cruise crucifying
                              our effort finally piercing through into
our memory the audience share of a spectacular
                              and newsable suicide final sum
of human knowledge of us mankind extinct gender
                              of us humans generated used scrapped

(if I talk to you now I don't talk to me, if I talk to me now
                              I don't talk to you and if I talk about it trust me
it's simply because the pining for bygone days
                              lingers in the breath elided in musings)

It won't last long so, won't last, won't last, I tell you
                              it won't last long so: here one starves
and dies from obesity one dies from wealth and poverty,
                              one dies from loneliness and noise one dies

in nome di Dio per liberarsi di Dio si
>   muore per il solo gusto di farlo e sentirsi anche
solo per un attimo Dio e io che qui trafitto
>   stringo al petto tutto il mio disfatto me
straccio il contratto e già tremo nel tirare
>   il dado credetemi vedrete che alla fine della fine
saremo colpevoli nostro malgrado e
>   ci saranno fiumi inutili di sangue e inchiostro mostri
perché così non dura, non dura, non dura:
>   forse saranno gli uccelli o un brulicare d'insetti
o gli occhi stretti delle belve degli esseri
>   striscianti delle selve né ce ne saranno in salvo
ma ce ne saranno invece di feroci dal cuore
>   calvo e le mascelle strette a digrignarci le
colpe a morderci l'anima al garretto a
>   strapparci confessioni torturate dal privilegio a
dettare l'ultimo florilegio lo spasimo ironico
>   che con un rutto dirà punto e basta che
dell'ultimo distrutto farà monumento del lamento
>   sberleffo sentimento spento tormento

(se vi parlo ormai non mi parlo, se mi parlo
>   *ormai non vi parlo e se ne parlo credetemi*
è solo perché le parole sono il ritmo della riscossa
>   *insulto autismo acre che dà la scossa)*

Così finisce male, male, male, gli dico
>   che così finisce male: perché ormai non ci sono
più perché né parole adatte allo sbigottimento
>   né attimi d'innamoramento né voglia di
vento perché si vive di spavento contento
>   di buio a cinque stelle di corpi senza pelle di
cielo senza faville di mascelle serrate di
>   maschere clonate si vive d'ignominia e falsità e
il male è un'ovvietà un'abitudine è un luogo
>   comune un vestito rozzo e tozzo sul futuro

298

in the name of God to get rid of God one
                                    dies for the sheer fun of it and to feel even just
for one split second like God & I am here pierced
                                    the whole of my dishevelled self hugged
I tear the haggled deed & shudder before throwing
                                    the dice trust me you'll see at the end of the end
we shall be to blame despite ourselves and
                            there shall be useless blood and ink rivers monsters
because it won't last long so, won't last, won't last:
                                    likely the birds or swarming insects
or the slit eyes of the savage of creeping beings
                                    in the foliage nor will anyone be salvaged
but there will be fierce ones instead
                            bald-hearted and jaws tightened to gnash our
guilts to nip our soul at the hocks to
                            tear confessions from us tortured by immunity to
dictate the last anthology the ironic
                            spasm that will say that's that with a hiccup that
will erect a monument to the last smashup to the lament
                            banter sentiment extinguished torment

(if I talk to you all now I don't talk to me, if I talk to me
                            now I don't talk to you all and if I talk about it trust me
it's simply because words are the rhythm of payback
                            insult bitter autism that gives you a whack)

It's gonna go wrong so, wrong, wrong, I tell him
                            it's gonna go wrong so: because now there are no
longer why's nor words suited to the dismay
                            nor instants of foreplay nor lust for
mistral because one lives on mortal fear blissful
                            with first-class darkness with a skin-less carcass with
a spark-less sky with clenched jaws on
                            xeroxed masks one lives on disgrace and falsity and
evil is blatancy a habit a cliché a nasty and
                            chunky dress on the future

299

un muro duro e scuro scudo transazione emozionale
investimento sentimentale senza sale
perché così finisce male, male, male:
e non vale il trucco dell'opulenza né quello bieco
della scienza non vale il Dow Jones che sale
non vale la conquista dello spazio e nemmeno
la commozione per lo strazio né le viscere
immolate all'eterna sordità del cielo solo forse
strappando il velo forse scavando fino alle radici
del melo e del canto comune dell'aspro pelo
e del gastrico gonfio di gas e bugie gonfio di
cibo e bolo e chimo e chilo dopo chilo dimagrirsi
il profitto sino a renderlo esistenza scommessa
rischio di utopia respiro lungo e promessa

(se gli parlo ormai non mi parlo, se mi parlo
ormai non gli parlo e se ne parlo credimi
è solo perché odio dire io l'avevo detto,
perché non c'è scampo e scampo non c'è se l'ho detto)

Così non va così non dura così finisce male:
c'è un'aria che spira un'atmosfera da strage
un clima che intima gente che plaude prona s'inchina
c'è che chi dovrebbe opporsi pone
domande e non ha risposte c'è che nessuno
ha più speranze riposte ma solo azioni e buoni
bontà in borsino e sentimenti in finanziera
c'è che è una mal'aria tutta umida di violenza e
senza ripari a cui correre né santi a cui ricorrere
c'è che anche i tuoi occhi ormai non vedono
quanto ciechi sono divenuti i miei vecchi di dolore
e di ore presbiti di anni e orbi di debiti
perché così non va così non dura così finisce male:
non c'è più sale nemmeno a fare male
solo cocci di bicchieri frantumi di piatti aguzzi
feroci come voci colli di bottiglia miglia e

a bitter and somber barrier emotional transaction

                                           sentimental investment feeble
because it's gonna go wrong so, wrong, wrong:

                    and the opulence trick is unfair like the grim one
of science the gleeful Dow Jones is unfair

                           the conquest of the universe is unfair like
the emotion for the curse like the entrails

                offered to the eternal deafness of the sky the odds are
that only by tearing the shroud maybe by digging to the roots

                       of the apple tree and of the common
coarse grain chant and of the gas & lies-bloated gut bloated with

             food & bolus & chyme & pound after pound trim
the gains so they're turned into existence a bet you can't hedge

                   Utopian risk long breath and pledge

(if I talk to him now I don't talk to me, if I talk to me

              now I don't talk to him and if I talk about it believe me it's
just 'cause I hate to say I told you so,

          'cause there's no way out & no way out of here if I told you so)

That's not good won't last long so will go wrong so:

                 bloodshed's in the air a stifling atmosphere
a climate that dictates people who acclaim prostrate

               they stoop fact is those who should resist ask
questions and have no answers fact is no one

          has any entrusted hopes but only actions and kindness
vouchers in the dealing room and feelings in a suit

              fact is it's a bad air all damp with violence and
no sheltering to run to nor saints we can have recourse

             to fact is even your eyes now no longer see
how blind mine have become old with pain

          and hours presbyopian with years and blind with debts
because that's not good it won't last long so it's gonna go wrong so:

                  there's no salt not even to hurt
just shards of glasses splinters of plates sharp

             fierce like voices bottlenecks miles and

miglia di parole e parole e parole resti d'ossa
        senza morsi torsi d'uomini e donne gonne
vuote di gambe mani senza braccia piedi senza
        dita solo quest'interminabile parodia di vita
sgradita senza uscita questo tronco d'esistenza
        che non fa più resistenza che s'arrende ma
poi già domani si pente pensa per vizio per
        abitudine che forse è possibile credibile immaginabile
che raschia il fondo si nutre d'avanzi e scampoli
        e sogni e intanto avanza avanza come un'onda
come un vento come un rigo che copre con la lana
        dei versi il corpo nudo di noi due, riversi…

miles of words and words and words remains of bones
                    with no bites torsos of men and women skirts
devoid of legs arm-less hands toe-less
                    feet just this interminable parody of life
unwelcome no way out this trunk of existence
                    that no longer offers resistance that gives up but
then tomorrow already repents it thinks out of vice out of
                    habit that perhaps it is possible credible imaginable
that scrapes the bottom feeds on leftovers and scraps
                    and dreams and meanwhile it moves on and on like a wave
like a wind like a line covering with a fleece
                    rhymed with twine the naked body of us two, supine...

Translation by Susanna Maggioni

Acknowledgements

The editor and publisher gratefully acknowledge permission to reprint copyright material in this book as follows:

ANTONELLA ANEDDA: 'VI' from *Notti di pace occidentale*, Rome, Donzelli, 1999; 'Esilii', 'Lacrime' and 'Anatomia' from *Historiae*, Turin, Einaudi, 2018. Translated by Jamie McKendrick. 'Limba' from *Dal balcone del corpo*, Milan, Mondadori, 2007. The poems 'VI' and 'Limba' are from *Archipelago*, London, Bloodaxe, 2014. Edited and translated by Jamie McKendrick.

FRANCO BUFFONI: 'Vorrei parlare a questa mia foto' from *Il profilo del Rosa*, Milan, Mondadori, 2000. Translated by Moira Egan, 'I'd like to talk to this photo of me', *Columbia Journal*, 9 November 2018. 'Da Marte dio crudo della Guerra' from *Guerra*, Milan, Mondadori 2005. Translated by Geoffrey Brock, 'Mars cruel god of war', *Poetry*, December 2007. 'Al canto in cerchio sincopato' from *Poesie 1975–2012*, Milan, Mondadori, 2012. Translated by Justin Vitiello, 'To the English Language', *World Literature Today*, Spring 1997. '"Sodomito," vergo un giovane collega' from *Roma*, Modena, Guanda, 2009. Translated by Jacob S. D. Blakesley. 'Com'era il mondo dove sbarcò Enea' from *Roma*, Modena, Guanda, 2009. Translated by Jacob S. D. Blakesley.

DOME BULFARO: 'Colonna vertebrale. Reperto n° 9', 'Carnificazione. Contatto n° 0', 'Tallone del capogiro. Contatto n° 25 (parte dx)' and 'Nuca. Contatto n° 31 (parte dx)' from *Ossa Carne (Bones Flesh);* bilingual edition Dot.Com Press, Milano, 2012. 'Ictus 1. Scheletrico di una famiglia' from *Prima degli occhi*, Monza, Mille Gru, 2015. All poems are translated by Cristina Viti.

MARIA GRAZIA CALANDRONE: 'Intelletto d'amore', 'L'85 è il sorriso degli amanti quando s'incontrano per caso a Fiumicino Aeroporto', 'Pietro Maso. Senza emozione e senza rimorso', 'sembrava una faccenda naturale, che tu nascessi, coi muscoli crociati in posizione' and 'Un misterioso albero-motore' from *Giardino della gioia*, Milan, Mondadori, 2019. All poems are translated by Johanna Bishop.

CHANDRA LIVIA CANDIANI: 'Dare la svolta' from *La domanda della sete 2016–2020*, Turin, Einaudi, 2020. 'Vorrei guardare il mondo' from *Fatti vivo*,

Turin, Einaudi, 2017. 'Ora sei trasfigurata' and 'Amo il bianco tra le parole' from *La Bambina Pugile*, Turin, Einaudi, 2014. All poems are translated by Bhikkhu Abhinando.

MILO DE ANGELIS: 'Milano era asfalto, asfalto liquefatto', 'Non è più dato', 'Tutto era già in cammino', 'Non c'era più tempo' and 'Il luogo era immobile, la parola scura' from *Tema dell'addio*, Milan, Mondadori, 2005. All poems have been originally published in *Theme of Farewell and After-Poems* by University of Chicago Press, 2013. The editors and translators are Patrizio Ceccagnoli and Susan Stewart.

MATTEO FANTUZZI: 'La Stazione di Bologna', 'Il senso di una strage' and 'Adesso questi volti sono tutti familiari' from *La stazione di Bologna*, Bologna, Feltrinelli, 2017. All poems are translated by Lara Ferrini.

SHIRIN RAMZANALI FAZEL: 'Love letter to my hometown', 'Afka hooyo-Mother Tongue', 'Stubbornness', 'Shambles' and 'Shamble' are self-translated and appear in *Ali Spezzate*, 2018, by Shirin Ramzanali Fazel.

FABIO FRANZIN: 'Marta l'à quarantatrè àni' from *El coeór dee paròe*, Zone Editore, 2000. 'Me despiase' and 'Artù' from *Fabrica e altre poesie*, Ladolfi Editore, 2013. 'No l'é pecà a ragàr' and 'L'é drio inbrunìr' from *Corpo dea realtà*, Puntoacapo, 2019. All poems are translated by Cristina Viti.

MARCO GIOVENALE: 'riga (una: un) picco voltaico' and 'già alle sette, a luce iniziata' from *La casa esposta*, Firenze, Le Lettere, 2007. Translation by Jennifer Scappettone, *Aufgabe* no. 7, 2008. 'book' is a poem originally written in English and published in *Capitalism Nature Socialism*, vol. 22, issue 1, March 2011 and Marco Giovenale, *anachronisms*, Ahsahta Press 2014. Translated by the author for www.gammm.org, https://gammm.org/2014/04/21/4-from-anachromisms-marco-giovenale-2014/. 'è molto facile contrarre la malattia' from *Erano in pericolo* published 2009, as well as *Quasi tutti*, Rome, Polìmata, 2010, and Turin, Miraggi, 2018. Translated by Linh Dinh, *Ekleksographia*, wave two, Sept. 2009 and *Moss Trill*, 2015.

MARIANGELA GUALTIERI: 'Sii dolce con me' from *Bestia di Gioia*, Turin, Einaudi, 2010. Translated by Anthony Molino. 'Ormai è sazio di ferite e di cielo' from *Le giovani parole*, Turin, Einaudi, 2015. Translated by Cristina Viti. 'Sono stata una ragazza nel roseto' and 'La miglior cosa da fare stamattina' from *Le giovani parole*. Translated by Anthony Molino. All translations by A. Molino and C. Viti come from Mariangela Gualtieri, *Beast of Joy: Selected Poems*, New York, Chelsea editions, 2018. 'Per tutte le costole bastonate e rotte' from *Bestia di Gioia*. Translated by Olivia E. Sears.

ANDREA INGLESE: 'Il contorno, che prende tre lati solo, è a meandri con fondi', 'Cornice in racemi popolati da miriadi di animali', 'In questa poesia/la distruzione arriva molto lentamente', 'In questa poesia/avvenimenti accadono alle persone' and 'In questa poesia/per salire sulla magnolia servono bambini', and from *La grande anitra*, Salerno, Oèdipus, 2013. All poems are translated by Johanna Bishop.

ROSARIA LO RUSSO: 'Le cose, bistrattate dai molti sgomberi', 'Così ci rubano – rimetta – l'antica lingua', 'Otturare le crepe, cremare i cadaveri', 'Dicevo insomma' and 'Irreparabilmente puerili grandi occhi' from *Crolli*, Firenze, Le Lettere, 2012. All poems are translated by Serena Todesco and William Wall.

VALERIO MAGRELLI: 'Scivola la penna' and 'Di sera quando è poca la luce' from *Ora serrata retinae*, Bologna Feltrinelli, 1980. Translated by Anthony Molino, *Nearsights*, Graywolf Press, 1991. 'Che la materia provochi il contagio', 'L'abbraccio' and L'imballatore' from *Esercizi di tiptologia*, Mondadori, 1992. The English versions of the poems ('That matter engenders contagion', 'The Embrace', and 'Removals Man') are in Valerio Magrelli's *The Embrace: Selected Poems*, translated by Jamie McKendrick, Faber & Faber, 2009.

GUIDO MAZZONI: 'Essere con gli altri' and 'Étoile' from *La pura superficie*, Donzelli, 2017. Translated by Dylan Joseph Montanari. 'Sedici soldati siriani' and 'Quattro superfici' from *La pura superficie*. Translated by Jacob Blakesley.

UMBERTO PIERSANTI: 'L'isola' from *I luoghi persi*, Turin, Einaudi, 1994. 'Lo stradino', 'La giostra', 'Figlio per sempre' and 'Oggi e ieri' from *Nel tempo che precede*, Turin, Einaudi, 2002. All poems are translated by Matthew F. Rusnak.

LAURA PUGNO: 'Vedi il suo corpo che tira di scherma', 'Serie con kayak', 'Non è la stessa lingua che parli', 'Più avanti, se la lingua è condivisa' and 'Apri la scatola nera' from *Il colore oro*, Firenze, Le Lettere, 2007. All poems are translated by Craig Arnold.

IDA TRAVI: 'Chi sono i Tolki', '(*il muso*)', '(*lo schermo parla chiaro*)', '(*l'animale*)' and '(*presto*)' from *Tasàr animale sotto la neve*, Moretti & Vitali, 2018, fifth book in the *Talki i parlanti* series (2011–2018). All poems translated by Alexandra Wilk and Tommaso Gorla.

LUIGI TRUCILLO: 'Lamiere' and 'The tube' from *Lezione di tenebra*, Cronopio, 2007. Translated by Martin Corless-Smith and Patricio Ferrari. 'Casa estrema', 'Per Ethel Rosenberg, presunta spia comunista' and 'Giorni e luce' from *Altre amorose*, Macerata, Quodlibet, 2017. Translated by James Schwarten.

PATRIZIA VALDUGA: Poems '8', '17', '45', '47' and '71' from *Cento Quartine*, Einaudi, 1997. Poems '107', '122', '124' and '154' from *Quartine: Seconda centuria*, Einaudi, 2001. All poems are translated by Geoffrey Brock and first published in *The FSG Book of 20th-Century Italian Poetry*, United States, Farrar, Straus and Giroux, 2015.

GIOVANNA CRISTINA VIVINETTO: 'La prima perdita furono le mani', 'La seconda perdita fu la luce', 'La terza perdita fu il perdono', 'Accadde che le ombre della mia infanzia' from *Dolore*, Minimo, Novara, Interlinea, 2018. All poems are translated by Cristina Viti.

LELLO VOCE: 'Lai del ragionare esperto', taken from *Piccola cucina cannibale*, (Squi[libri], Rome, 2012) is translated by Susanna Maggioni.

PARTHIAN *Poetry in Translation*

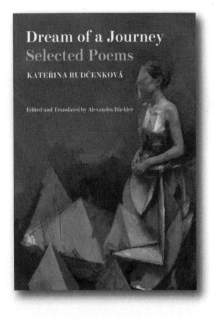

Dream of a Journey
Selected Poems
Kateřina Rudčenková
Edited and Translated by Alexandra Büchler
ISBN 978-1-913640-54-5
£10 | Paperback

'A mix of romanticism, existentialism,
absurd drama. Simply great poetry.'
– **Radim Kopáč, *Týdeník Rozhla***

Odetta in Babylon
and the Canada Express
Gregorio Kohon
Translated by Gregorio Kohon
with Toni Griffiths

Introduction by
Gwen MacKeith

ISBN 978-1-913640-51-4

£9 | Paperback

'It's terrific…a mysterious involvement with
the deepest things – life, death, love, failure,
aspiration, youth, sensuality, knowledge…'
– **Melanie Hart**

PARTHIAN *Poetry in Translation*

Home on the Move
Two poems go on a journey
Edited by Manuela Perteghella
and Ricarda Vidal
ISBN 978-1-912681-46-4
£8.99 | Paperback
'One of the most inventive and necessary
poetry projects of recent years…'
– Chris McCabe

Pomegranate Garden
A selection of poems by Haydar Ergülen
Edited by Mel Kenne, Saliha Paker
and Caroline Stockford
ISBN 978-1-912681-42-6
£8.99 | Paperback
'A major poet who rises from [his] roots to touch
on what is human at its most stripped-down,
vulnerable and universal…'
– Michel Cassir, *L'Harmattan*

Modern Bengali Poetry
Desire for Fire
Arunava Sinha
ISBN 978-1-912681-22-8
£11.99 | Paperback
This volume celebrates over one hundred years
of poetry from the two Bengals represented
by over fifty different poets.